GHOSTS AND LEGENDS OF SPOKANE

D1604124

GHOSTS
AND LEGENDS
OF SPOKANE

DEBORAH CUYLE

FOREWORD BY MARK PORTER

Haunted
America

Published by Haunted America
A Division of The History Press
Charleston, SC
www.historypress.com

Front cover: The Davenport Hotel.

First published 2021

Manufactured in the United States

ISBN 9781467146357

Library of Congress Control Number: 2021938362

Notice: The information in this book is true and complete to the best of our knowledge. It is offered without guarantee on the part of the author or The History Press. The author and The History Press disclaim all liability in connection with the use of this book.

DEDICATION

Why do they say ghosts are cold? Mine are warm, a breath dampening your cheek, a voice when you thought you were alone.
——Julie Buntin, Marlena

I dedicate this book to my incredible son, Dane Brown, who has always been my best friend and cohort in the passion for writing and anything scary. Also, to my wonderful Middy, who never complains when I am writing nonstop even though a yummy dinner and a couple cold cocktails are waiting for me to share with him. My appreciation also goes to all my BFFs who have joined me in a little ghost hunting now and then and support my paranormal research and beliefs. An open mind is an open door. I personally have experienced so many unexplained things that I cannot explain that I can no longer even remotely doubt the existence of ghosts or spirits. In fact, the century-plus-year-old home I am living in now in the quaint old silver mining town of Wallace—an hour from Spokane—is extremely haunted by two friendly ghosts.

And last but not least, to my incredible and loving mom, Roxine, who always believed I could do whatever I set my mind to do. I swear she somehow still visits my sisters and me in times of sorrow or if we are just missing her.

My books are also dedicated to all of my fellow ghost hunters out there. Without them, I would be wandering around dark rooms all by myself with my EMF detector and my cellphone application Ghost Radar...and that wouldn't be very much fun at all.

Happy ghost hunting!
Deb

CONTENTS

CONTENTS

FOREWORD

The dead are watching, whether or not we choose to listen to their stories.
— *Colin Dickey,* Ghostland: An American History in Haunted Places

Considering the length of time Eastern Washington has been settled by Euro-Americans, there is a considerable amount of paranormal activity throughout this region. As cofounder of the Spokane Paranormal Society, I have seen, heard and felt many unknown instances where our team could not find reason for what has just happened. This area has had its fair share of natural events, hauntings both positive and negative, and atrocities committed by settlers and government against the Native Americans of the nineteenth and twentieth centuries.

Deborah has the unique ability of presenting the unique history with experiences and lore of the locals to convey to her readers just how the place she is writing about is seen.

This book will delve into the Spokane area to give you a firsthand knowledge of the history and events from the stately manors in Browne's Edition and Upper South Hill to the formative years of the Downtown region and the working man's residences in Hillyard, the Lower South Hill and the East Side.

Much of the area will start to take shape from the Indian Wars of Eastern Washington and running through the mining barons and industrial age. Many of Spokane's elite of the early 1900s have their mansions talked about by the people of Spokane, as the haunted happenings documented here. As someone who has investigated many of them, I can tell you in my opinion, yes, they are most definitely haunted! This is my personal opinion.

By the end of this book, you will not only understand better the history of Spokane and how it came to be but also strange things that do happen in its historical places. Chapters will fly by, people from the past will stick in your head and the stories of some of those people from after they have passed away will truly amaze you. You have yourself a memorable read you will come back to more than once.

For now, grab a beverage, find a comfortable spot and turn your phone off. It is time to immerse yourself in the world of *Ghosts and Legends of Spokane*!

—Mark Porter

PREFACE

Maybe all the people who say ghosts don't exist
are just afraid to admit that they do.
—*Michael Ende,* The Neverending Story

I hope readers visit many of these sites as they learn about the fascinating history of each of these haunted places. As is common with my books, I try to incorporate as many historical facts, names and dates as possible in each chapter. I feel this brings the ghosts and their stories to life and makes learning about the towns more interesting.

Many of my readers tell me they enjoy both aspects—learning about the town's history while reading about the local ghosts that haunt the buildings. Teachers and parents both contact me to thank me, stating that many of their students and children are *not* interested in local history at all but that they love to read about it in my books. For this I am grateful and hope to continue to enrich their minds and hopefully open up a world that they will find both fascinating and interesting!

I love hearing a good ghost story, and after researching the building, I can actually find evidence of someone with that name who actually lived at that location (or died there) at one time or another.

Being a NDE (near death experience) survivor, I am probably a little more open-minded than most people. Perhaps someday science can prove what really happens to us after we die—the eternal mystery questioned by every living being—but until the riddle is solved, it is all just speculation. Religion and science may someday agree, but they likely will not. I see both sides of the debate. Too many unexplained events happen to each of us to not entertain the idea of ghosts and the spirit world. I read somewhere that God or spirits do give us signs when we ask for them, but we, as humans, are too busy or too close-minded to see them or recognize them. I often wonder what life would be like if people were not so skeptical of the possibility of the spirit world. How would that change the way people behave in this world today? Would it be reassuring or terrifying to most people? I am often baffled by people who tell me that they believe in the afterlife but not in spirits. How can the two really be separated? Perhaps some dead people just choose to haunt a place while other spirits choose not to? It is a wonderful mystery.

This recent book project exists because I have great interest and respect for the early pioneers and a fascination for local history and old buildings. I love all the lore and legends that ghosts and spirit storytellers have shared with me. It is fun to walk the same streets today that early settlers once walked and think of how it was back in the old days. Imagine the pioneers who trekked to Washington with little more than a dream, a horse and a few dollars—only to soon become one of the listed millionaires! When I look at old brick buildings or original hardwood floors, I try to envision the thousands of people who once walked these streets or visited these buildings, the horses that pulled wagons and goods, the gunslingers and outlaws, the bartenders and shopkeepers—all of them living their lives and going about their business, just as we all do today. I would have loved to have been alive in the late 1800s!

History is full of people who haunt us, who want to be recognized and never forgotten for what they accomplished while alive—the improvements they created for a town or what they offered their family and community. This book is about those fascinating spirits—the spirited people who made Spokane what it is today.

Most of the stories were told to me by locals, and some have been pulled out of old newspapers—all told out of fun for the love of history and lore. Some of the buildings in this book are no longer (or never were) haunted, but I have included them because they had such a big impact on Spokane's history and/or the buildings themselves have significant architectural importance and it would be a shame to not include them. Of the many towns I have written about, Spokane has the most incredible and amazing rags-to-riches and architectural history of all. I am always in wonder at the beauty of the buildings of Spokane as I drive I-90; I have to be super careful so I don't rear-end someone…so many of them are mind-boggling amazing!

PREFACE

The book is *not* intended to be a nonfiction project, and even after hundreds of hours hunched over reading and researching, I still found conflicting dates and inconsistent historic details—so please take it for what it is and enjoy the book. I tried to be as accurate with names, dates and details as possible, but this is mostly a book full of tales of many mischievous ghosts and the interesting history of Spokane.

ACKNOWLEDGEMENTS

There are many people to thank for this endeavor, and without their help and guidance, this book would not have been possible. My wonderful editor, Laurie Krill, has been such a pleasure to work with, along with all of the other incredible people at Arcadia Publishing and The History Press. Their mission to promote local history is passionate and infectious, and I am blessed to work on my books with them. Their dedication to recording local history and people's stories is remarkable, and without them, many books would never be published.

My appreciation is also extended to all those who took the time to share their personal ghost stories and experiences—without them this book would not have the extra flair that I love so much. Mark Porter of Spokane Paranormal Society has been a fun and knowledgeable person to explore places with and learn so much about Spokane's haunting history.

And as always, I want to thank every single person who does what they can to preserve history—whether it is volunteering at the local historical society, maintaining old cemeteries and gravestones that would otherwise be neglected or simply researching their private genealogy and personal history through great sites like Ancestry.com. In this fast-paced and high-tech world, the past can unfortunately be easily forgotten, and every effort to maintain and record valuable data, photographs, diaries, documents and records is of the upmost importance for future generations. I urge people to take the time to learn more about and explore (if allowed) the many fascinating locations in this book and the people who participated in developing them.

ACKNOWLEDGEMENTS

One final request, please do not disturb or trespass on any of the locations listed throughout this book without permission from the property or business owners, as some have experienced property destruction and littering, and this is unfortunate. Thank you for understanding.

INTRODUCTION

In the realm of haunted cities, Spokane, Washington, is high on the list, with countless ghost-infested old buildings and spooky places to visit. Platted by James Glover in 1878 when it was just a half-dozen log cabins, Spokane soon shot to a population of over 100,000 people by 1910. It attracted a cluster of rich men and was quickly considered the "wealthiest city in America" with over 20 millionaires (and 28 half millionaires) living there. But with the financial glory and the many rags-to-riches scenarios also came some dreadful consequences. Murders, disputes and suicides—all lend to the plethora of ghosts that haunt the city till this day. Patsy Clark, mining millionaire, and his wife, Mary, refuse to leave their fourteen-thousand-square-foot mansion, and Mary's ghost is often seen dressed up ready to enjoy another extravagant party. At the grand Davenport Hotel, the spirit of a woman named Ellen who accidentally plunged to her death from a skylight to the marble floor below still whispers, "Where did I go?" to guests. The ghost of the original owner himself, Louis Davenport, can often be heard roaming the halls at 3:00 a.m.—his usual time to walk around and check on his magnificent hotel and his beloved guests. The "one thousand" frightening stairs at the Greenwood Cemetery attracted hundreds each year to see if they could get "blocked" by spirits while ascending to the top of the crumbling steps. The suicidal wife of the "Mad Doctor of South Hill" remains restless in their Hahn Mansion, where she was found dead with a fatal bullet to her head. Tenants of the Helena Apartments (once managed by serial killer Stanley Pietrzak) claim to hear faint screams from the basement, where he once tortured and killed a woman.

Spokane is filled with an excess of haunts and is a well-known Washington paranormal hot spot. The century-old streets are brimming with spooky buildings and the restless spirits that continue to roam the city—never wanting to leave their favorite town, situated by the nearby beautiful Spokane River. The city's history and mansions are as interesting as the ghosts themselves. And as you walk the streets and observe the old buildings, think of the early pioneers who came from all over the world to make Spokane their home.

Many spirits are still living there, unwilling to leave—why would they want to?

Spokane's History

Spokane is one of the most fascinating cities in Washington. Its history is rich in many more ways than just old money and mansions. But back in the day, if you were lucky enough to become a prominent and wealthy citizen of Washington State, you lived in Spokane!

Although Spokane was a fast-growing area in the 1900s, it experienced its share of tragedies and setbacks. Founded by James Nettle Glover in 1873, the town consisted of a mere half-dozen log cabins, a few shacks and several canvas tents. Yet Glover was not wrong in his foretelling that the area would soon be booming with activity and people. The town was originally called Spokan Falls, and in 1883 the *e* was added. Then in 1891, the "Falls" was dropped, creating the name known today—Spokane.

One of the first large hotels to be built in Spokane was the California House on Front and Howard Streets, and the proprietor was W.C. Gray. In 1881, the Northern Pacific Railway brought into Spokane a large number of immigrants eager to work, and they continued to come to the area for work for many years. In 1886, the first brick hotel was built, the Arlington—a four-story beauty on Howard and Main Streets. Many more hotels were to follow—to house workers as well as tourists.

One of the worst tragedies for early Spokane was the Great Fire that burst out in August 1889 (it started by the Northern Pacific Railway tracks and raged ravenously for a stressful thirty-six hours) and quickly spread until it completely destroyed a whopping thirty-two city blocks. The firemen were

Above: The California House was one of the first hotels built after fire, 1878. *Washington State Archives.*

Opposite: The blackened Glover block after a fire in which some lost their lives, 1889. *Spokane Public Library, Northwest Room.*

not successful due to the fact that the pump station was not working properly and the men had no water pressure to douse the flames. Once the flames were controlled and eventually stopped, the town's people and business owners were devastated. A man named George Davis was killed. The rumor was the fire had started in Wolfe's lunchroom near the depot. The estimated loss of property was between $5 and $10 million.

Due to this devastating event, the city quickly installed electric fire alarms and created a paid fire department with horse-drawn carriages. But Spokane made a miraculous recovery, and by 1890 over five hundred new building had been erected. The first hotel to be built after the fire was the Merchant on West Riverside. The second one was the Pacific on the corner of Howard and Main Streets. The Hotel Spokane was damaged by the fire but rebuilt into a first-class hotel with an astonishing two hundred rooms.

But soon Spokane and the world were hit with another tragedy: the Spanish flu epidemic during World War I (1914–1918). Many hotels were used for makeshift hospitals and morgues, including the Ruby Hotel, among others. Over eleven thousand Spokane residents were stricken with

influenza, and over one thousand of its residents died. Closures and masks were required to help slow down the spread of the disease. Recovery was slow, but soon Spokane was on the road to recovery on many levels. Spokane citizens were determined to rebuild their communities and businesses. The city still had such a tremendous draw—its beauty and location by the water—that many people flocked to it like moths to a flame.

Just as Glover had probably predicted, Spokane would have tremendous population spikes even during its horrific fire and life-altering pandemic. The population tripled—going from 36,000 people to 104,000 in just a few years. In 1908, over three thousand business and building permits were issued, and Spokane became second only to Chicago. In 1909, the first skyscraper towered high into the air: the eleven-story Paulsen Building. That same year, the Bakke-Mugstad Building went up at Browne and Pacific with 160 rooms boasting "running water and closets in every room!" During this time, Spokane was to become home to fourteen millionaires. By the end of 1910, the *Wenatchee Daily World* reported that "133 residents of Spokane own property total valued at $58,000,000 and has twenty-six millionaires, making Spokane one of the wealthiest cities in the country."

The *Spokane Daily Chronicle* listed the millionaires: "J.J. Browne, Amasa Campbell, F. Lewis Clark, Patrick "Patsy" Clark, D.C. Corbin, William Cowles, Louis Davenport, John Finch, Jay Graves, Frank Hogan, M.E. Hay, L.W. Hutton, Aaron Kuhn, August Paulsen, Col. Peyton, among others." Some of these men truly had rags-to-riches inspirational stories in their past.

Mansions were being built in Spokane with millions of dollars of railroad and mining money—beautiful, luxurious estates that still remain today. Some haunted, some not, but all are a part of Spokane's rich and fascinating history.

Spokane is currently a mix of both old and new buildings, all nestled closely together in an assortment of styles and sizes. When touring Spokane's streets, suddenly an enormous hotel, home or building comes into sight and reminds the viewer just how majestic and exquisite the city of Spokane has been for over one hundred years.

1

HAUNTED MANSIONS

I think if I believe in anything, I believe in ghosts.
—Alice Hoffman, Skylight Confessions

PATSY CLARK MANSION

Too Glorious to Leave

A ghost story from Lila of Spokane:
Everyone knows the Patsy Clark mansion is haunted....One time when I
was younger me and a group of kids from school all decided to hang out in
the park area near the house and see if we could experience anything. The
house was not being lived in at the time. As we sat there for what seemed like
forever, we were all about to give up and go home. Just about then I could
swear I saw a figure moving through the house, like a dark shadow moving
past the windows inside! I am sure it was a trick of the eye or something,
maybe from a passing car, but to me it was a ghost and I always wondered
if it was the man who built it still keeping an eye on his place. I would if
I was him, it's still so pretty.

The Patsy Clark mansion located at 2208 West Second Avenue (across
from Coeur d'Alene Park in Browne's Addition) is well known to be one
of the most haunted places in Spokane, as apparitions of a female ghost

The beautiful, haunted Patsy Clark Mansion today—with no gargoyles displayed on the exterior. *Author's collection.*

wearing all-white attire is frequently seen walking down the stairs in the foyer. Many believe this is the ghost of Mary Clark herself, who refuses to leave her beloved and beautiful estate. While living, Mary was said to host elaborate and elegant parties to entertain Spokane's elite crowd. Of Mary Clark, it was written: "Beloved by people in all walks of life, Mrs. Clark has been part of the heartbeat of Spokane's civic, social, and charitable life for five decades. It does not fall to the lot of many to leave such a beautiful heritage."

Patsy and Mary were generous throughout their lives in Spokane, aiding many in need as well as helping with the construction of certain buildings. They contributed to the completion of Our Lady of the Lourdes Cathedral in 1900, and later (after Patsy's death) Mary aided in the construction of the Sacred Heart Hospital. It is no wonder their spirits remain in Spokane, especially at their grand estate.

Today, piano music can still be heard when there is no apparent source for the melodies. The hauntings reportedly started around the same time the home was converted to a restaurant called the Francis Lester Inn. There was

A peek inside one of the formal rooms at the grand Patsy Clark mansion. *Author's collection.*

a lot of paranormal activity in the wine cellar of the basement. Although all reports of activity remain positive and friendly, it is believed that Mary may not have been pleased with the conversion of her home. Renovations are a sure-fire way to stir up the spirits.

A lot of the paranormal activity began in the 1980s during the remodeling into the new Patsy Clark Restaurant. The restaurant was so elegant that even President George H.W. Bush dined there in 1989. It is well known that ghosts don't appreciate disturbance. Many employees saw the ghost of Mary and experienced the sensation of being watched and followed and hearing music. Down in the old wine cellar, bottles of wine would float in the air or be tossed across the room.

It is interesting to note that the original home was designed with several gargoyles attached to its exterior. Gargoyles are believed to ward off evil spirits. A symbol from France, they are often thought to protect against harmful spirits. They have been used in architecture for hundreds of years. Did Patsy Clark know something secret about the land he was going to build his house on, have private superstitions or simply enjoy the statues?

A portrait of Patsy Clark still hangs above one of the many fireplaces in the home, and some report his eyes follow you as you walk by. Is Clark still keeping watch over his mansion? *Author's collection.*

The gargoyles could have had a more innocent design—they are often used to convey water from the side of a building to minimize the erosion created from rainwater. Since the Patsy Clark mansion was built in the rainy state of Washington, this may certainly be the case. The world will never know.

The lavish Spokane home of Patrick "Patsy" Clark (1852–1915) was designed in 1897 by famous local architect Kirtland Kelsey Cutter (1860–1939) and finally completed in 1889. The 11,422-square-foot, three-and-a-half-story, nine-bedroom/five-bathroom home also had nine onyx fireplaces. The mansion cost $13 million to build, and Clark spared no expense during its construction. Cutter was ordered to create the "most luxurious mansion *ever*" and "the most impressive home west of the Mississippi" personally by Clark. And Cutter performed as asked. Examples? The exterior sepia sandstone was imported all the way from Italy, and an extravagant grandfather clock from England that cost a whopping $17,000 resided in the lavish home. The walls were adorned with beautiful Spanish leather, hand-stamped with

The stairwell where the floating image of the beautiful Mrs. Clark can often be seen walking down the grand stairs toward the landing. Her beloved Tiffany window can be seen in the background. *Author's collection.*

Patsy Clark spared no expense when building his estate, and every room is still picture perfect. *Author's collection.*

designs, and the dining room was embellished with rare Egyptian gopher wood. It was all over-the-top in design, and no expense was spared. Once neglected and destined for the demolition ball, it has been lovingly restored and is again a subject of extreme beauty.

The two-story, fourteen-foot-tall stained-glass windows and chandeliers were special ordered from Louis Comfort Tiffany (1848–1933), the famous American stained glass and jewelry designer in New York City. The wall coverings were imported from an 1800s German monastery. Mary Clark enjoyed luxurious gold-lined chairs, delicate silk curtains and even a gorgeous, expensive rug in the library. The estate also boasts spectacular turrets, arcaded porches and a carriage house. One of the most breathtaking features in the home is a huge eight-by-fourteen-foot stained-glass piece at the head of the stairs with a beautiful Art Nouveau peacock motif. It was said the home furnishings alone cost Clark a small fortune.

A ghost story from Mark Porter from Spokane Paranormal Society:
We were investigating the Patsy Clark mansion, and the most haunted
object is the old grandfather clock. It was not working at the time. When

we got close to the clock, our gauges would light up. Something was affecting our equipment. When we moved to the second floor, we saw a cigar box, clip and matches in Patsy's card room. That was the only room in the house he was allowed to smoke. We smelled sulfur, and when we looked one match was lit and the end was charred. We were the only people in the room! Nobody else was in the room. The third floor of the mansion was the boys' rooms—it is very active. We gathered many EMFs there.

Patsy was born in Ireland on St. Patrick's Day in March 17, 1852, and came to America at the young age of eighteen aboard the SS *Marathon*. In 1876, he began working the mines in Butte, Montana, where he also met his lovely wife, Mary Stack. For good luck, they wed on St. Patrick's Day 1881, and together they had six children. In 1888, they moved to Spokane, Washington, where Clark opened the Poorman Gold Mine in the Coeur d'Alenes with partner Marcus Daly. The men later sold this mine for a wonderful profit. Clark then teamed up with a group of prosperous men (Finch, Campbell, Wakefield and Corbin) and invested in mines in British

The Patsy Clark mansion used to have several gargoyles above the exterior arches to ward off evil spirits. The gargoyles were removed during renovations. *Spokane Public Library.*

Columbia. To keep even busier, Clark developed the Republic Mine, which became one of the richest in Washington and British Columbia. A lucky man, indeed!

Clark would go on to become one of the richest men in Spokane. The Clarks continued to live happily in their mansion until their deaths—Patsy in 1915 and Mary in 1926.

The mansion went through several enterprises over the next few decades. An investor named Eugene Enloe purchased the home in 1950, but by the 1970s the building had deteriorated and sadly barely escaped demolition. In 1975, the much-deserving building was listed in the National Register of Historic Places.

Next it became the Francis Lester Inn, which operated until 1982. It was then sold and reopened as the Patsy Clark Restaurant and operated as such for twenty years. It was then sold again to the law firm of Eymann, Allison, Hunter and Jones, which faithfully restored the once beautiful home to its original glory. Still owned by the law firm, the Patsy Clark mansion is up for sale for $2.1 million. Who will be the next lucky owner of such a beautiful and elegant building?

Attorney Richard Eymann commented, "It [the building's renovations] was worth the investment. This building is almost sacred to Spokane. Some people believe it is haunted, too, by the ghost of Mary Clark, widow of Patsy Clark."

No one knows what the next phase of the Clark mansion's history will be, but one thing is for certain: the Clarks may never leave their beloved home in the Browne's Addition Historic District. Why would they? It is one of the most beautiful homes in all of Spokane.

Note: A link about the mansion can be found at: www.kxly.com/the-patsy-clark-mansion-now-has-a-list-price-2-1-million/

The Corbin Mansions

Some say the Corbin mansions are haunted; others insist they are not and never have been. But the mansions are so gorgeous and significant to Spokane's history, it would be a shame not to include them. A book about

Spokane would not be complete without the story of an amazing pioneer by the name of Daniel Chase Corbin (1832–1918). His private mansion at 507 West Seventh Avenue is now the Corbin Arts Center. Once located on a four-and-a-half-acre parcel overlooking Spokane on the Marycliff–Cliff Park area, the incredible Georgian Revival estate was built in 1898 by Corbin's former son-in-law, the famous local architect Kirkland Kelsey Cutter. (Cutter was married for a brief time to Corbin's second daughter, Mary, and they had one son, Kirkland Corbin Cutter.)

Daniel Corbin was born in Newport, New Hampshire, in 1832, and in 1860 married Louisa Jackson. They had three children: Austin, Louise and Mary. A few years later, he made his way west to Spokane, and his sharp business mind soon made him a fortune. In 1893, Corbin purchased a former fairground at an auction and turned it into the Corbin Park Addition.

He took note that the area needed transportation for the rapidly growing mining districts, so he built a railroad line that catered to this need. He also created a line of steamboats for the same purpose. Corbin continued to grow his business, and in 1905 he built the Spokane International Railway connecting Spokane with lower Canada. In 1908, Corbin developed the Corbin Coal and Coke Mine Company to move the coal from British Columbia.

The magnificent D.C. Corbin mansion built in 1898 is now the Corbin Arts Center. *Author's collection.*

The magnificent home built for Corbin cost him $17,000, but all his money and beautiful home did not buy his happiness. Unfortunately, his wife, Louisa, and three children never got to enjoy the estate. Louisa did not care for Spokane and instead kept their family tucked away in Europe.

In Europe, daughter Mary fell in love with Kirkland Kelsey Cutter. Cutter studied in New York and then traveled to Europe to continue his education in Paris and Florence. Their brief marriage ended, and Mary later married an English nobleman named Edward Balguy of London.

Kirkland Cutter made his way to Spokane, Washington, in 1886 to work at the First National Bank with his uncle, Horace Cutter. But banking did not suit Cutter, and soon he was practicing architecture and (possibly with his dad's influence) began designing mansions for wealthy mine owners. He became one of the most prominent architects in the area, designing most of the homes on Seventh Avenue (including the mansion for Austin Corbin in 1898).

Daniel Corbin died on June 29, 1918. The spectacular mansion then became property of his second wife, Anna. It is possible Anna herself roams the glorious estate, as she loved its beauty and elegance. The spectacular view of Spokane would bring back memories of her loving husband's accomplishments and all he did to help create the city.

The First National Bank on the southwest corner of Front and Howard, circa 1883. *Spokane Public Library, NWR.*

The incredible Austin Corbin House is now offices for local businesses and events. *Author's collection.*

What spirit would wish to leave such a fine home? It has a beautiful wraparound porch with elegant Doric columns and above the entry a grand porch in which to take in the city's view. The house is perched under a basalt cliff of rocks on the lower south hill. Many of these large rocks form fences, gates and unusual and interesting landscaping all around the area. The home boasts Palladian windows and dormers, leaded glass windows, brass chandeliers, oak pocket doors, fluted column fireplaces, ornamental wood carvings on the newel posts on the banister railing and handsome cast-iron radiators.

Perhaps to earn income or perhaps to have company, Anna decided to alter the home in 1933, when she began taking in boarders.

In August 1945, Anna sold the property to the Spokane Park Board for the sum of $15,000; it was later turned over to the city and developed as a much-needed arts center. In 1963, the building became the official home for the Corbin House of Arts and Crafts and offices for the Spokane Parks Department.

In 1992, the Corbin mansion was listed in the National Register of Historic Places. It has been lovingly restored and remains a truly magnificent testament to Cutter's architectural abilities and Corbin's historical significance to Spokane's development.

The other Corbin mansion is located nearby at 815 West Seventh Avenue and was built for Corbin's son, Austin, in 1898. The mansion, with its towering columns and elegant, beautiful details, is now used for events and office spaces. There are no reports of paranormal activity, but it is included in this book due to its architectural beauty and significant Spokane history. It is known today as the Historic Corbin Mansion Events Center.

THE CAMPBELL HOUSE

The Campbell House is reportedly haunted by several entities and possibly a few children. There have been many apparitions of young children playing on the grounds and in the home as well as strange noises. Icy cold spots can be felt throughout the mansion, and the eyes in the portrait of an original owner, Amasa Basaliel Campbell (1845–1912), are said to follow you as you walk by. Some say there is a female spirit that resides in the upstairs sewing room. Paranormal groups have recorded high EMF readings throughout the home. A ghost has been seen numerous times in the old carriage house. Many people just feel like they are being followed or watched while in the home.

The rumors that in the early 1900s three of the Campbell children were murdered in the home and a fourth one kidnapped by a burglar (never to be returned) are all over the internet. This may be part of the hype of the phantom children playing there, but after much research, not a single article or any evidence of the Campbells having any children other than Helen can be found. A man as prominent as Campbell would get a lot of publicity over such a scandal. Regardless, the home is notoriously haunted, but the main possibility is that the Campbells themselves do not want to leave their gorgeous mansion.

The grand home at 2316 First Avenue in Spokane's historic Browne's Addition was built in 1898 at a cost of $75,000 for self-made millionaire Amasa Campbell; his wife, Grace; and daughter, Helen, by legendary architects Kirkland Cutter and Karl Malmgren. Campbell made his millions in mining with his partner John Ayland Finch (1852–1915).

The Campbell house is reportedly haunted and one of the last mansions that is open to the public. *Author's collection.*

The formal dining room in the luxurious Campbell mansion, where some have seen apparitions. *Spokane Public Library, photographer Harlon Betts.*

But the men were not always wealthy. Campbell was one of ten kids and never knew his father. At age twenty-two, he left his home in Ohio and began working for the Union Pacific Railroad. In 1871, he invested in a mine in Utah. In 1887, he took a job working as a scouting agent for wealthy speculators from Ohio. Around this time, he met his lifelong friend John Finch. The men were both sent to the Coeur d'Alenes in search of investments and to investigate the Coeur d'Alene mining region operations. At the time, Campbell was forty-two years old and had recently worked for a freight terminal. Finch was an unemployed salesman for a failing iron mill. Neither of them could ever imagine that someday they would both be two of the richest men in Spokane.

Neither man had any real mining experience, but they were great thinkers. Their plan? Whenever a mine hit a good vein, they immediately invested in any nearby mines, knowing that the vein could certainly travel to other areas. The plan worked! In a true rags-to-riches story, the men soon became rich beyond their wildest dreams.

Campbell married Grace Fox and then moved to Wallace, Idaho, in 1890; there they built one of the town's most prominent mansions on the corner of Third and Cedar. (The home still exists today and is just as remarkable now as it was back then).

The men invested in the Gem Mine, made some money and then moved ahead with the Standard Mine. Soon they were able to build the famous Hecla Mine in Burke, Idaho, in 1891. (Burke is now almost a ghost town, but many Hecla Mine buildings can still be seen from the road.) Campbell was president of both the Standard and Hecla Mines. His partner Finch invested in many other business adventures—of which he always made Campbell vice president.

After several dangerous mining disputes in Wallace, Campbell decided to move his family to the safety of Spokane in 1898 and build another, even grander mansion. Campbell's 13,600-square-foot English Tudor–style estate had a service wing and a carriage house. Built during Spokane's famed "Age of Elegance," it boasted a basement that was for playing poker and pool and a grand gold reception room. The reception room was done in a French rococo style and had a gold and onyx fireplace (one of ten), rose moiré silk wall coverings and gold leaf moldings.

Later, in 1925, their only daughter, Helen Campbell, gave the spectacular house to the Eastern Washington State Historical Society as a loving memorial to her mother. Amasa Campbell died of throat cancer in 1912 at the age of sixty-six, and Grace died in 1924. Both Amasa and Grace are buried at the haunted Greenwood Cemetery in Spokane.

The beautiful Grace Campbell stares out a window in her mansion. It is rumored she does not want to leave her exquisite estate. *NW Museum of Arts & Culture, purchased by author.*

NOTES: The Campbell Mansion was donated by Helen to the Eastern Washington State Historical Society and the Cheney Cowles Museum. It is open to the public. The house sometimes hosts "Halloween at the Campbell House," featuring trick or treating for children, and has also been featured on KXLY TV. There is an amazing collection of vintage photographs to view or purchase online at the Northwest Museum of Arts and Culture website: www.ferrisarchives.northwestmuseum.org—search under "Campbell."

Best friends for life John Aylard Finch built his own Georgian Revival–style mansion two doors down from Campbell for his wife, Charlotte, and their three servants in 1898. Located at 2340 First Avenue, the spectacular home has four three-foot-wide Ionic columns decorating its sixty-foot front façade and even had its own art gallery. The Finch family lived in their elegant mansion until 1915.

The Finch mansion is not reported to be haunted, merely a beautiful testament to the many pioneers who made their way in Spokane. He made a fortune as developer of the Hecla Mine and spared no expense when building his home, also designed by the famed architect Kirkland Cutter.

Upon viewing the mansion, the first glance shows a towering sixty-foot façade with a two-story portico that has four three-foot-thick Ionic columns. The intricate leaded-glass windows are spectacular throughout the home. When entering the home, the foyer extended twenty feet wide and held many beautiful paintings, with other paintings hung in the adjoining art gallery. The Finches were proud of their art collection. Unfortunately, after World War I, most were sold or auctioned off along with their furniture in the early 1920s.

The majestic Finch Mansion in Browne's Addition (to the left of the Campbell mansion) as seen in 1898. *Washington State Archives.*

Finch was born in England in 1854 and traveled with his family to Ohio when just a young boy. Later, in 1881, he got involved in some mining operations in Colorado. Six years later, he transferred his interests to the Coeur d'Alene region and partnered with friend Amasa Campbell. The two men developed both the Gem and Standard Mines, but the most productive mine they held was the Hecla Mine in Burke. The Hecla made both Finch and Campbell wealthy.

Finch married Charlotte Swingler in 1896 and became actively involved in early Spokane's development. He was generous and donated both money and land to the city. The incredible mansion was listed in the National Register in 1976.

NOTE: The Finch Mansion is a private residence. Please respect the residents' privacy by remaining on the sidewalk as you enjoy viewing this beautiful historic home. The Finch home is *not* reported to be haunted but is a fascinating part of the architectural history of Spokane.

HAHN–WILBUR MANSION

A Mad Doctor and a Suicide

A ghost story from Alice:
Have you ever heard your name being called out to you, as clear as day, when you know for a fact you are the only person in the room? So many times I have heard someone call my name and when I turn to respond or see who it is—no one is there. Who is doing this? I have read that it is an unexplained phenomenon. Is it ghosts? Loved ones? I wish I knew.

Once home of the "Mad Doctor of South Hill," the Hahn-Wilbur Mansion is said to be haunted by his wife, who supposedly committed suicide in the home in 1940. Although the house is now a private residence located at 2525 Nineteenth Avenue, former ghost hunters told the author that the sounds of gunshots, arguing, anguished cries and phantom parties and loud music could be heard when no one else was in the home.

All of these paranormal noises make sense once the strange and creepy history of the home on Nineteenth Avenue is revealed.

One of the few photographs of the "Mad Doctor" Hahn and his wife, Sylvia, who tragically committed suicide in their mansion. *NW Museum of Arts & Culture, purchased by author.*

The sprawling home was originally built by a couple named Ralston Wilbur and Sarah Smith. Smith had inherited her previous husband's money when he died, leaving her a small fortune. Her deceased husband, John Smith, was a leading shareholder in a productive Burke, Idaho mine called the Hecla. In 1908, on his passing, Sarah had to start a new life.

She did this in 1916 with a man named Ralson Wilbur, and together they spent Smith's money to build a home on Spokane's South Hill. They hired local legendary architects Gustav Pehrson and Kirtland Cutter to build their $75,000 (over $2 million in today's money) mansion. The *Spokesman Review* reported in 1916 that Sarah said the following of her marriage to Wilbur:

> *It was my intention to leave for Chicago as soon as the railroad situation was settled, with the object of closing up my affairs there and returning to Spokane to get married and make my home there. Mr. Wilbur would not consent to this program and insisted, since he could not get away from his business, that we be married today. I really did not have anything to say about it. He just rushed me over to the courthouse and secured a license. The wedding followed in such quick order that the hotel people did not even know we had been married.*

Was it true love, or did Wilbur have an ulterior motive? The world may never know...

The Craftsman-style home was built in the side of a hill and lavishly adorned with massive stonework, huge boulders, a Japanese meditation garden, mother-of-pearl inlays, a beautiful arched stone bridge, intricately carved doorways (with a vine pattern painted in gold leaf) and four large Chinese lanterns in the living room. The house was situated on a little over three acres on South Hill.

But all of this elegant luxury did not make the couple happy, and they divorced soon after the construction of the home was complete. In 1919, they sold the home to a Spokane pharmacist named William T. Whitlock, but even he only lived in the house for five years.

It was later sold to a self-absorbed and eccentric man named Rudolf Albert Hahn (1865–1946) from Chicago. Recently divorced from his first wife, the fifty-three-year-old "doctor" married a twenty-one-year-old girl named Sylvia D. Fly (1898–1940) in 1933. Sylvia was a beautiful woman from Colfax, Washington, and fly away she should have done.

Throughout the marriage, Hahn bullied Sylvia and enjoyed scaring her. Although he was technically licensed, he never really went to medical school to be a doctor. His preferred choice of medical administration was performing illegal abortions and providing electroshock therapy to his patients. He also spent lots of money to build an underground tunnel from his home to the nearby garage—so his patients could enter the home in privacy for their "treatments" and stay out of the public's leering eyes.

Hahn was known to throw extravagant and drunken parties during which he would play ridiculously loud music to the irritation of his neighbors. He wore absurdly expensive suits while his feet were clad in mere bedroom slippers. One of the most bizarre habits he had? He would shoot his guns *inside* the home. His target? Insects.

The day his wife died, the investigating officers found that the interior walls were riddled with bullet holes when they arrived on that fateful May 2, 1940, after Hahn had called them to report the death of his wife.

The police found poor Sylvia dead in her bed with a gunshot wound to her head. Apparently, Sylvia had a history of suicidal threats, but did she really go through with it this time? It was noted in the coroner's report that there *was* some evidence of gunshot residue on her hands. The *Evening Star* reported on May 7: The Coroner concluded that indeed Mrs. Hahn was killed by a "self-inflicted gunshot wound."

It took only thirty-eight minutes (after only three hours of testimony) for the jurors to decide it was suicide. Sylvia was forty-two years old at the time of her death and Hahn was seventy-four. Hahn testified under oath that he had "heard the doorbell then heard a gunshot and ran to find his wife dead."

Hahn sold the home in 1945 because he felt he could not live in the home anymore without his wife. He was later charged with unrelated manslaughter after his involvement in a complicated legal tangle. A patient from Mullen, Idaho, died on his operating table after he performed one of his illegal abortions. Although found guilty, he was only ordered by the judge to "no longer practice medicine." Since Hahn was eighty-one years old, the judge just gave him a fine and placed him on probation—clearly, he was too old to put in jail. Or so the judge thought. It was a tragic end to an already tragic fate for the young female victim who trusted him for her private care.

After the sale of the mansion in Lincoln Heights, Hahn moved into the New Madison Hotel in Spokane, located on the corner of First and Madison. A year later, on August 6, 1946, Hahn innocently answered the door to his apartment to find a hearing aid salesman named Delbert Visger standing there. The true story will never be known, but a fight ensued and somehow Visger got a hold of one of Hahn's World War II bayonets and stabbed him in the heart. Some believe the stabbing was revenge for a botched abortion of Visger's loved one a few years before. How many other victims died at Hahn's hands?

The Hahns are both cremated and strangely stored together at the Fairmount Memorial Park in Spokane. The decision for their bodies to be stowed side by side might seem odd, but somehow the couple is together for eternity in their joint urns.

Is it possible the mansion is haunted by the unhappy Sylvia? Or is it Hahn himself wanting to return to happier times—the years in which they lavishly entertained guests and threw loud parties in their elaborate estate? One will never know who lurks in the former Hahn home.

NOTE: The Hahn-Wilbur Mansion is privately owned, and the owners DO NOT wish to be bothered by any ghost hunting, curiosity seekers or any other form of attention. Please respect their wishes and do not disturb them or trespass on the property. More info on the property can be found at: https://properties.historicspokane.org/property/?PropertyID=1973

GLOVER MANSION

A Vision of Beauty

This incredible twelve-thousand-square-foot mansion at 321 West Eighth Avenue was built in 1888 by one of Spokane's original "fathers," James Nettle Glover (1837–1921). Spokane was platted by Glover in 1878 with just a half-dozen log cabins nestled in the area, but the settlement's population climbed to over 100,000 people by 1910, attracting many wealthy men to the area.

Although the residence is now used for amazing and beautiful wedding venues and is reported to *not* be haunted, others claim it might be haunted by the vengeful Susan Glover herself, Glover's first wife, whom he left on the sidewalk one day with nothing more than a suitcase. (Susan was later committed to a mental ward.) Mrs. Glover is said to still roam the Greenwood Cemetery for some unknown reason.

Haunted or not, the history of Glover and his mansion is fascinating. The glorious mansion is so spectacular that a book about Spokane's history would not be complete with it—and Mr. Glover's story. He is known for being a big contributor to early Spokane's social and commercial development.

Glover, a real estate millionaire, married Susan Tabitha Crump (1843–1921) in Salem, Oregon, on September 1, 1868. They moved to Spokane from Portland in 1873. They divorced in 1892 for unknown reasons, and just days later, Glover remarried a younger woman named Esther Emily

Mr. and Mrs. James Glover together in their beautiful home. *Spokane Public Library.*

Leslie (1859–1924). Susan was sent to a mental ward, where she sadly stayed twenty-two years until her death. Does the scorned Susan haunt her old mansion? Or is it someone else who roams its halls? Some contractors who have worked on the home in prior years report of tools being moved and objects disappearing. Legend tells that when the workmen were putting in a new heating system, a box was found with the name "ANN" written on it, and some of the hidden objects were in the box. The apparition of a little girl has been seen running up and down the halls as well as slamming doors. Could this be the ghost of Ann? Who was Ann? A mystery never solved.

Glover came to Spokane in 1873 and he created the first general store in Spokane as well as the First National Bank. He also became the second mayor of Spokane.

The mansion was the first major architectural effort of Kirtland Cutter and the real push to his incredible career. The three-story, English Tudor–style, twenty-room mansion cost $100,000 to build in 1888. The glorious home had eight bedrooms, five bathrooms, a carriage porch, a beautiful stone arch on 250 feet of Eighth Avenue frontage, a two-story-high mezzanine

Mr. and Mrs. James Nettle Glover relaxing in their mansion in Spokane. *Washington State Digital Archives, AR-07809001-ph00425.*

inside, elaborate carved stairways and specially made furniture to fit each room individually. Other interior details include intricate lion heads carved into the marble fireplace and beautiful leaded glass windows. The third floor even held space for twelve servants. The mansion was a magnificent Spokane showpiece.

But the glory was not long-lived. Glover lost a fortune in the financial Panic of 1893, along with many other prominent men of Spokane. (During the Panic of 1893, unfortunately seven out of every ten banks closed their doors, causing terrible losses.) In 1898, he sold the home to Frank H. Graves, a prominent lawyer in town. The Graves family lived peacefully in the mansion until 1904. Sadly, the significant "Father of Spokane" moved to a small home on Summit Boulevard, where he lived until his death in 1921.

The next owner would be Charles Sweeney (a U.S. deputy marshal and mine owner), who lived there for four years until he died in 1908. Spokane felt heavy sorrow at the loss of Sweeney, as he was well respected and loved in the community.

The beautiful Glover mansion had twenty rooms and twelve servants. *Washington State Archives.*

The mansion was then sold to the Patrick Welch family in 1908 for just $80,000. Welch was a contractor for the railroad and greatly responsible for the tracks on both the Canadian and U.S. borders. He was involved in construction all over the world, including Canada, Africa, Great Britain, Persia and Spain. When he died in 1929, construction stopped briefly on his projects in a final tribute of respect and honor to such a great man. The Welch family continued to enjoy the estate, living there happily until 1934.

In 1934, it was sold to the Unitarian Universalist Church of Spokane for services and office spaces until 1992. During the 1990s, it was used as an event center until it was sold again as a private residence. The significance of the Glover mansion in Spokane's history is of great value. It was the "first estate of its kind to be placed on the National Register of Historical Places" in 1973.

No one truly knows who was haunting the mansion or if it is even still haunted, but one thing is certain: it remains one of the most spectacular and gorgeous homes to ever be built in Spokane.

NOTES: The Glover Mansion is *not* currently reported to be haunted; instead, it is known as a big part of the fascinating history of Spokane. Please respect the owner's privacy by remaining on the sidewalk as you enjoy the beauty of this historic building. Please do not disturb the business at this location unless you plan on holding a wedding or event there in honor of its beauty and elegance. Ghost hunting is not allowed!

A detailed account about James Glover can be found through the Washington Biographies Project in October 2015 by Diane Wright at: http://jtenlen. drizzlehosting.com/WABios/jnglover.html.

2

HAUNTED BUILDINGS

It's possible that the reason I've never experienced a ghostly presence is that my temporal lobes aren't wired for it. It could well be that the main difference between skeptics (Susan Blackmore notwithstanding) and believers is the neural structure they were born with. But the question still remains: Are these people whose EMF-influenced brains alert them to "presences" picking up something real that the rest of us can't pick up, or are they hallucinating? Here again, we must end with the Big Shrug, a statue of which is being erected on the lawn outside my office.
—*Mary Roach*, Spook: Science Tackles the Afterlife

A ghost story, Anonymous:
I bought my house in 1997. It was August. I remember it because it coincided with Princess Diana's death, and the first thing I watched on TV in my home was her funeral. The couple who owned my house were Alan and Vivian. Vivian was the last to go. She did not die in the home; she was in a care facility. I'm not sure about her husband, Alan. I was in the home for a few years, somewhere around four years, when I started to notice a strong cigarette smell. I don't know why it didn't come to me sooner. When I bought the house, the girlfriend I had at the time had a toddler, and he was really active, so I probably was so overwhelmed with him and her that I didn't have time to notice anything else in the world! About four years into the home, I had a new partner, Mary. She had asked me early on in our relationship if I smoked, to which I replied, "Never." And she commented that she often smelled cigarettes in my home, but it was intermittent.

One day we were sitting downstairs watching TV; it was around 6:00 p.m. I remember it was summertime because I had a window open. Suddenly, we both smelled cigarette smoke, and we both commented on it at the same time. It was not just a small smell, it was overwhelming. I started to cough, a lot; my face was turning red, and I had to get out of the room. I staggered upstairs, and I went outside. I thought for a minute maybe someone blew cigarette smoke into the house from outside. I staggered over to the side of the house where the window was open. No one was there. After a couple minutes I went back in, and Mary helped me get up the stairs. My lungs were burning; it was like someone just blew smoke in our faces.

The next couple weeks later, I was standing in front of my fridge. This time I was by myself in the house. Suddenly, in front of my fridge it was an artic wind or something just *happened* in front of the fridge. It was STRAIGHT out of a movie. I exhaled, and I could see my exhalation, like you do when its outside in the cold. This too made my lungs burn. I suffer from asthma, so sudden exposure to cold can trigger it. I started coughing again, and I fell to the floor. The air went back to normal, and I felt better after a few minutes. This freaked me out, and I immediately called my friend Faye, who is a psychic. I wasn't into the whole ghost thing, didn't really have an opinion one way or the other. But, at this point, picking myself up off of my own floor in the middle of the day, in the middle of summer, something wasn't right.

Faye came over, and right away she said Alan told her he was NOT leaving. Vivian was apparently sad and said she missed her family. I asked Faye if she could talk with these two entities and see if we could coexist. It's a three-level house—perhaps there could be room for all of us? Plus, they gave me asthma, so could they keep their distance from me in particular? Faye went up into the top level of the house, and she was up there for about an hour. She said they agreed to not come close to me, and she said they would mainly stay upstairs. About five years ago, say 2015, Vivian's son came by the house, and he asked if he could come inside. I let him inside, and we talked about all the remodeling I had done. After he left, I noticed something different about the house—it's hard to explain, but I'm pretty sure Vivian left with him. I have not smelled cigarette smoke since then. Alan may be gone too; he doesn't bump around in the night like he used to. For the last several years it's been REALLY quiet here. I've been here almost twenty-three years this summer. This home was a Sear's kit home, built in 1922. It's a great house, and I can see why someone would hate to leave. That's my ghost story!

Hillyard Variety Store/Spokantiques

A question from the owner: Do we have spirits in our building? My husband says something is going on here!

This is a fascinating store in the downtown historic Hillyard district at 5009 North Market Street where people can find almost anything. It is loaded with everything from vintage furniture and household goods to an early 1900s sewing machine to a caned Spanish Colonial bench. With so many antiques, it is no wonder there might be a spirit or two walking around. Some believe material objects can hold spirits if the previous owners loved the item so much they do not want anyone else to have it or they just cherished it while they were alive.

A ghost story from Grace, who purchased a vintage chair:
I bought an old chair that I instantly fell in love with that needed some TLC and to be reupholstered. I took it home and began cleaning and sanding it, removing the old material, etc...One night as I came down to my basement to work on the chair I saw what appeared to be an older gentleman sitting in it. At first I was startled, but he simply looked up from his newspaper and smiled at me—then he vanished. It actually made me happy because I could visualize this man enjoying his chair every morning while reading his paper and having coffee. I said aloud, "I don't know who you are, but I hope you like what I plan on doing to your favorite chair! I am going to freshen it up and give it a new look. I will keep you in mind when I pick out the new fabric for the seat." I made good on my promise....When it was time to pick out the fabric I chose a more masculine design in honor of the spirit I saw. I never saw him again, but in my heart I know he is probably happy with my choice.

Psychometry is the term used by psychics who can sense an object's history by touching the item. Through a form of ESP, they can pick up and transfer the memories or knowledge from the energies that are attached to it. This is one form of valuable psychic phenomenon that can be utilized by police investigations searching for missing persons.

Mark Porter and Raymond Lusk of the Spokane Paranormal Society did an investigation at Hillyard Variety Store/Spokantiques on July 10, 2019.

NOTE: View their investigations on their Facebook page: https://www. facebook.com/page/1688984644710881/search/?q=Hillyard

A ghost story from Mark Porter of Spokane Paranormal Society:
We investigated the Hillyard Variety Store on several occasions. There are apartments upstairs that have several entities lingering, many of which were trapped and needed our help. One was named Big Pete. We patiently helped them to cross over and leave the building. We communicated with seven spirits, several of which unfortunately had committed suicide. One spirit was a man in his late twenties possibly thirties that hung himself. He told us he had a grocery store below and had experienced financial troubles and that he just couldn't handle the pressure anymore.

We encountered a rather funny and entreating gentleman who went by the name "Edwin" who told us he was a homosexual and that he loved to visit the drag shows across the way! We discovered that he also liked to "touch" people jokingly. At one point he rubbed my leg and I said, "Uhm, Edwin, I am happily married, my partner here is happily married...but my friend over there (pointing to another friend) now he is single!" The psychic that was with us said he got a big kick out of that comment and she could hear Edwin laughing!

The old area of Hillyard goes way back in Spokane's history—dating back to the late 1890s—so it is no wonder the neighborhood has a lot of ghosts. The neighborhood has retained most of its original buildings, which respectfully earned its listing in both the Spokane Historic Register and the National Register of Historic Places. Walk around, and hopefully you will experience a ghost or two.

BING CROSBY THEATER

Two Spirits Decide to Stay

Some accounts say the building is haunted while others discount the idea, but it has been acknowledged by KREM news and local ghost historian Chet Caskey. Is the theater at 901 West Sprague Avenue being haunted? If so, by whom or what? It is said Bing haunts other nearby buildings, but who is to say a spirit cannot roam from place to place? Especially if those places are some of the ghosts' "happy spots" while they were alive?

The Bing Crosby Theater is supposedly haunted by two spirits. The first is a former stage manager who had an unexpected heart attack while

The Bing Crosby Theater is supposedly haunted, although Bing himself haunts other Spokane locations. *Author's collection.*

backstage. The second ghost is that of a young girl from the early 1920s. The story goes that she was in love with a boy who was supposed to meet her at the theater in 1924 and they were going to elope. After waiting for her love (who never showed up), she was so distraught and heartbroken that she flung herself from the high balcony and committed suicide. Her hazy spirit can be seen occasionally pacing the balcony as if still waiting for her lover's arrival.

Harry Lillis Crosby (1903–1977), commonly known as "Bing" Crosby, was a well-loved singer and actor who originally enrolled in Spokane's Gonzaga University in 1920 to study law. He was born in Tacoma, Washington, but his family moved to Spokane when he was just a few years old. His childhood home is still standing in Spokane, and this is where his love of music began. He developed his nickname when a neighbor began calling the boy "Bingo from Bingville" (from a comic strip) and the name stuck.

One of his most popular songs, "White Christmas," sold over 100 million copies. In his career, he had over 300 hit singles. Bing gave his final Spokane performance at the theater before making his way to Hollywood.

A peek inside the wonderful Bing Crosby Theater where two ghosts roam. *Author's collection.*

The theater, designed by architect Edwin Houghton (1856–1927), was originally called the Lincoln and the Paulsen, as it was built by August Paulsen. Paulsen had made his fortune in the Idaho silver mines, along with many other men. He quickly moved to Spokane and became a developer. The parcel situated next to the grand Davenport Hotel was the perfect spot for him to build a deluxe movie theater. So he did. Its doors opened in 1915 during the beginning of the new age of motion pictures. It was grand, with ornamental plasterwork and hand-painted landscape murals on the walls painted by I. Peterson (who also did the murals in the Davenport Hotel). The auditorium could hold 300 guests and the balcony above another 450 people. One of the most fascinating architectural feats for the theater is its coffered vault ceiling, designed as an acoustic shell to accommodate the melodies from the three-thousand-pipe Kimball organ. This would be the first type of acoustic vault design for any theater and the first of such organs to be installed in the Northwest.

The theater had no one to run it yet, but that all changed when its first lessee, Dr. Howard Clemmer, took on the project and changed the name to the Clemmer Theater. Dr. Clemmer was a former dentist who developed an interest in movies after his father's passing. His dad had built several small movie houses in Spokane and Seattle. Clemmer operated his theater until 1925.

The dazzling stage had 1,600 lightbulbs. In 1925, the building was sold to Universal Studios. At that time, the current manager thought it would be a good idea to offer live acts in between the movies to entertain customers. This is where Harry "Bing" Crosby entered the stage—literally. He was a local favorite jazz musician and hired right away. Over the years, the theater changed hands and names several times. In 1929–30 it was renamed the Audian when Ray Grombacher bought it, and in 1932 it changed names to the State Theater. It operated as the State Theater until 1985; it sat empty for a few years until a local mortgage company swooped it up and began updating and renovating the building. It reopened as the Metropolitan Theater of Performing Arts, or The Met for short. In 2004, the theater changed hands once again when a local businessman named Mitch Silver purchased it. In 2006, the building was renamed the Bing Crosby Theater, and it has been called that ever since.

Although Bing is not known to hang out and haunt the theater, it is possible his spirit pops in now and then, as it was one of his favorite local places to entertain hundreds of people.

NOTE: The spirit of Bing Crosby *is* said to haunt a nearby building: the Crosbyana room at the Crosby Student Center located at 508 West Sprague Avenue, where his Oscar from 1944 is displayed along with many other interesting and noteworthy memorabilia from Bing's life. It has been reported by some visitors that drum music can be heard when there is no one playing the drums. Bing was an excellent drummer. Bing died in 1977 during a golfing vacation in Spain of a massive heart attack. After playing a really good game at the La Moraleja course near Madrid, it was reported that Bing was in great spirits and showed no signs of fatigue. Some say his final words were, "That was a great round of golf, let's go get a Coke." His death shocked millions of fans. Does his fun-loving spirit hang around to enjoy the amazing collection of his personal items being displayed?

THE BUCHANAN BUILDING

A Former Funeral Home and Mortuary

A ghost story from Mark Porter of Spokane Paranormal Society:
We have investigated this building six times. The old viewing room is the most haunted. We had a medium with us, and when she entered the room she had an overwhelming urge to look up at the skylights and felt like crying. It makes sense because that would be the "view" from the corpse's perspective! A reporter was also with us, and we asked, "Can you give us a sign or make a sound?" Just them we heard a loud BANG! *He said, "I didn't believe in ghosts, but I do now!"*

When we went down to the basement, which was the old cold storage room for bodies, we saw a strange object in our camera in the hall area. It looked like a microscopic view of a germ—I don't know how else to describe it. The video clip showed it moving out from the window, down the wall and exit through the floor. It could not be the shadow or light bouncing from a car outside because in the basement there are NO cars.

The Buchanan Building at 28 West Third Avenue in the Riverside neighborhood has a good reason to be haunted. It used to be a mortuary.

James Daniel Buchanan (1858–1920) came to Spokane from Illinois with his wife, Ella, and their children in 1880 and started a cigar and tobacco shop. Buchanan later gave up the tobacco business for the more lucrative work of undertaking in 1898.

His new building was designed in 1911 by local architects F.P. Rooney and Lewis Stritesky; it was used specifically for his mortuary business until 1924. The building cost $25,000 to construct. During construction, Buchanan ran his business out of a building at West 310 Riverside Avenue. Originally, half of the building was used as a garage and stable, and the upstairs was a hayloft with a few apartments. The building has a beautiful Gothic-style tin ceiling and leaded glass French doors. Buchanan's undertaking establishment was considered one of the finest in Spokane.

Later, the Buchanan building became the Hennessey & Calloway Funeral Home until 1935. Since then, it has been the Spokane Funeral Home, a plumbing & heating company, a Goodwill store, a ceramic arts store and an antique store.

Although now it is a business center, it is said that ghosts still linger in the halls of this building. They have been seen in the old furnace room in the basement—where the closet used to be a coffin elevator.

NOTE: Please do not disturb any of the owners or tenants of this building, as it is currently being used as a business.

SPOKANE COURTHOUSE

The Ghosts of the Gallows

Many locals and paranormal investigators feel the old courthouse located at 1116 West Broadway is haunted by several entities. Using either special ghost hunting equipment or basic household flashlights, intelligent responses can be received from the spirits. Through the turning on and off of the flashlights or the displaying of words, the entities can answer simple questions for the investigators.

The Spokane County Courthouse around 1896. It is haunted by murderer Charles Brooks and a few other spirits. *Spokane Public Library, donated by Dr. Willis Merriam.*

The Brooks and Dohlman Murder

Many believe one of the ghosts that haunts the courthouse is that of a sixty-two-year-old Black man named Charles Brooks who murdered his estranged wife, twenty-seven-year-old Christine Dohlman, in cold blood. Brooks would have good right to be haunting the old courthouse, as he was the first person to be legally hanged in Spokane, in 1892, and is probably feeling remorse and guilt from beyond the grave.

Brooks was a small man, standing only five feet, three inches and was formerly enslaved in Mississippi before the Civil War. He suffered from a head injury from a bullet he received while serving in the Colored Regiment of Tennessee. Some attribute his murderous actions to this injury. Others do not.

Murderer Charles Brooks haunts the courthouse where he was hanged on March 30, 1900, for killing his wife in broad daylight. Brooks was the first Black man executed in the courthouse. *From the* Seattle-Post Intelligencer, *September 7, 1892.*

In happier times, he fell in love and asked for Christine's hand in marriage after only a few weeks of courting. But their marriage soon went on the fritz, as Brooks had promised Christine a life of wealth. He said he held over $30,000 in Spokane real estate (although in reality he was barely making a living as a janitor at the Webster house) and could provide a nice life for them. Christine soon found out otherwise. Frustrated that she had been misled, she filed for a divorce from Brooks in June 1891. Soon Brooks began threatening to kill her if she didn't return to him. Upon investigation, Brooks *did* hold money in real estate, but unfortunately, since he was illiterate, he had been cheated out of his land claims by his son-in-law in 1888. Brooks shot him in the neck in a rage after he found out about the incident.

One summer evening, July 5, 1891, Christine and her sister got together and decided to take a stroll—Brooks followed the women. He continued to follow Christine and her sister, Mrs. Moline (who also had her two children with her, keep in mind) as they were walking along the alley by the Penobscot Hotel on Havermale Island. Soon Brooks came up behind the women, startling and frightening them.

The *Seattle-Post Intelligencer* told the story on September 7: Brooks approached (Christine) Dohlman, and he said "I want to speak with you!"

and Dolman replied, "I don't want anything to do with you!" As the two women and the two children turned to walk away, Brooks pulled out his revolver and shot his wife in the back of the head. Then he fired another two shots. As Dohlman fell to the ground, she was still holding one of the children. The screaming Mrs. Moline hurriedly grabbed her child from the dying woman's arms and fled the scene. Brooks was reported to be calm and just remained standing over his wife's dying body.

Officer William Smith was patrolling nearby and, when he heard the shots, went running to the area, where he found the grisly scene. Brooks stood calmly with the gun still in his hand.

All Brooks said was, "You can take me and hang me now."

Which Spokane County was prepared to do.

Brooks was tried and convicted in October 1891 for killing his wife. It was appealed on the grounds of insanity due to his head injury. His appeal was denied by the Supreme Court, and he was sentenced to the gallows.

Sheriff Francis K. Pugh sent out 150 formal invitations to the citizens of Spokane to attend his hanging scheduled for September 6, 1892, at the Spokane Courthouse. In that era, it was strangely considered an honor to be invited to a public execution. When word got out, over 1,000 citizens crowded to the event, although they were not allowed inside the fence to actually see the hanging.

It was reported that Brooks was calm prior to the event, even participated in the singing of "When I Can Read My Title Clear." Then he smoked a cigar while walking on the path to his death trap. After the hood was placed over his head and the clock struck the designated time, the trap was released and Brooks died instantly.

It is no wonder that Brooks is haunting the old courthouse. Tragedy always creates trapped souls, unable to cross over until they are encouraged by the living or spiritual guides.

The strange part to the story is that Brooks is buried in an unmarked grave (no one offered to buy a plot or headstone for Brooks) at Spokane's Greenwood Memorial Terrace and that the body of Christine Dohlman was buried next to him for all eternity.

It is said that Christine's restless ghost walks the grounds of the cemetery at night, furious that she is buried next to her murderer. And perhaps Brooks is still begging for Christine's forgiveness at his inexcusable actions. Hopefully someday their souls can rest in peace.

NOTE: The graves of Brooks and Dohlman will remain unmarked, as the cemetery *does not want* any graffiti, vandalism or curious ghost hunters lurking about for their graves. Please be respectful. Images of their unmarked graves can be found online for the curious.

The Strange Homicide of Lise Asplund

Another possibility haunting the old courthouse is the ghost of the first white man (and last legally hanged person by Spokane County) to be hanged from the gallows in Spokane, George Webster (1871–1900). Ghost hunters have received words like *sorry*, *wrong* and *death* on their spirits boxes when investigating in the same area where the gallows were erected.

Webster was known as a laborer and handyman, considered hardworking and skilled. He had a hard life when young, as both parents died and he began to live on his own at the tender age of thirteen. He typically worked in the town of Cheney, near Spokane. In May 1897, twenty-six-year-old Webster was drinking in several saloons in Cheney until around 7:00 p.m. when Constable Brown politely asked Webster to leave town. The drunken Webster decided to slowly make his way by walking toward Medical Lake. Soon tired, Webster decided to try to find a place to sleep for the night.

A family by the name of Asplund had a small farm near Cheney. Andrew Asplund was originally from Sweden; he immigrated to America in 1877 and married Lise Holm (1852–1897) in 1882. On this particular night of May 6, the inebriated Webster knocked on the door of the Asplund farm and asked if he could bed there for the evening. The kind family took him in, not knowing that the evening's events would change their lives forever.

Andrew Asplund needed some help on the farm, so the men made an arrangement that Webster could stay and work a few days for the wage of seventy-five cents per day plus board. Agreeing, the men shook on it. After dinner, the family soon went off to bed. The men slept in the only bedroom, and Lise and her two small girls (Ella May, age thirteen, and Jennie, age eleven) were sleeping in the kitchen.

During the night, Webster got thirsty and asked for some water. Andrew Asplund let him know there was a bucket of drinking water on the porch. Webster made his way through the kitchen toward the porch. This is where things took a bad turn. Lise told the police officer later that he had stopped and tried to touch her girls. Of course, the angry mother urgently shooed him out the door. Webster apparently got his water and then returned to bed. Soon he decided he wanted some "medicine" (whiskey) and again left the bedroom. Around 2:30 a.m., Lise again shooed him away—this time locking him out of the house. When Webster tried the door and found it locked, he became angry and demanded his coat and hat, as he was leaving and making his way on to Medical Lake.

Lise, tired of the stranger, eagerly decided to give him his belongings so he could get on his way and out of their home. She put his hat and coat on the end of a broomstick and poked it out the kitchen window for him to retrieve. Lise thought she also saw a second man outside with Webster.

George Webster was the first and last white man to be hanged at the Spokane Courthouse and might still haunt it along with Brooks. *From the* Spokane Daily Chronicle, *March 30, 1900.*

Soon the loud bang of a gun being fired sounded through the air! Poor Lise was shot in the abdomen, the bullet lodging in her spine. Her girls watched in horror as their mother lay dying on the kitchen floor. Andrew woke at the sound of the gun shot and ran to the kitchen with their son, John, thirteen. As the family looked in shock at Lise bleeding at their feet, Webster wandered back in the house and asked who was shooting. Lise told her family that Webster had been the one who shot her.

Strangely, Webster casually walked back into the bedroom and went to sleep.

Panicked, Andrew ran to his neighbor William Spence's house and asked for help. Spence's son George was ordered to go fetch a doctor and the police in the nearby Cheney.

In Cheney, Constable Abel Brown (the very same one who had ordered Webster to leave his town earlier that day), town marshal John Corbett and Dr. Francis Pomeroy were quickly dispatched and made their way back to the Asplund farm in horse-drawn carriages.

It was around 5:00 a.m. when they arrived. Lise had gone back to bed in the kitchen, and oddly, Webster was still asleep in the bedroom as if nothing had happened.

When the marshal grabbed Webster to handcuff him, a .38-caliber revolver fell from his coat. He also had two pints of whiskey and several incriminating articles on him—all logged as evidence.

Lise identified Webster as the man who shot her before she was rushed to the hospital in Medical Lake. Unfortunately, the bullet wound had gone untreated for so many hours that it was infected and poor Lise died at 10:42 p.m. Friday night.

Once the word got out about what had happened to the Asplund family, a mob gathered at the jail and demanded Webster be lynched. Constable Brown moved Webster to avoid something happening to his prisoner.

On May 10, Webster was charged with first-degree murder and sentenced to death by hanging. Webster pleaded not guilty on May 14, and the trial was set for September 15, 1897.

It was recorded in the *Spokane Daily Chronicle* that Webster told Lise in front of witnesses, "Yes, I shot you. I don't know why I did it. I am very sorry, and I hope you get well."

Complications with jurors and votes made the trial convoluted. Besides Lise's testimony prior to her death, no one else could actually say *who* shot the gun. Was it Webster or the mysterious stranger also lurking outside the farm at 2:30 a.m.? Many believed Webster shot Lise in anger because she locked him out of the house to protect her children from his advances.

Webster was found guilty, and the execution date was scheduled for July 28, 1899, after several years of appeals and nonsense. He was to be hanged at the Spokane County Courthouse. But right before he was schedule to be executed, an extension of life was granted by U.S. District Judge Hanford.

For unknown reasons, six thousand people petitioned Governor Rogers for clemency but were refused. Execution clemency is a plea for mercy of a convicted person for an act of grace or pardon. Rogers held his ground, and the plea was never even considered. The people felt that life in prison was enough punishment for Webster, but his execution was put on the calendar.

Two hundred people were invited to attend the execution, and ten days before the scheduled hanging, the scaffold and platform were unpacked and started to be assembled. The trap door had a fifty-pound weight attached to the underside of it.

Webster claimed that he should not be convicted of a crime he did not remember committing. The Asplund family and many others felt otherwise.

On the morning of his execution, Webster requested toast, eggs and coffee as his last meal at 7:00 a.m. At 9:00 a.m., he was read his death sentence. At 11:00 a.m., he was led to the scaffold, where his final words were simply, "Goodbye."

His body was taken to Gilman & Company Undertaking and Parlors in Spokane at 308 Riverside Avenue. Webster is buried at the Greenwood

A gallows for hanging men similar to this one was used near the Spokane Courthouse. It was positioned in between the jail and the courthouse building. *Wikimedia Commons, public domain.*

Cemetery (now called Greenwood Memorial Terrace), where some say he sadly wanders the grounds hoping for forgiveness. Webster's execution cost Spokane County $896.90.

The Asplund family never truly recovered from the nightmare, and all of them ended up with severe mental issues that required institutionalism. It was a sad, tragic end for a family that was simply trying to help a stranger out.

The area where the scaffold was erected was between the courthouse and the jail—a common area known for paranormal activity today.

NOTE: Another curious rumor is that there is a hidden tunnel under the courthouse by the parking lot that ran from the old jail to the new one. The area where they once held executions on the makeshift gallows is now the customer service department area. Some employees have felt there is paranormal activity there, possibly the spirit of Brooks or some other restless spirit.

THE PIETSCH HOUSE

And a Nearby Unsolved Murder

Noted as the oldest home in the Peaceful Valley neighborhood, the two-story brick Pietsch (pronounce "peach") House had many past rumors of shadowy figures and eerie sounds coming from the building during the several decades it sat vacant. Nicknamed the "Ghost House," it is located at 1647 West Main Avenue. The home was built in 1891 by Franz Pietsch (1838–1914) who immigrated to Spokane from Germany with his wife, Augusta. Pietsch was born in 1838, came to America in 1867 and spent some time in Minnesota in an area known as Smith's Hill before heading to Spokane (after the Great Fire of 1889 that destroyed most of downtown Spokane). He was an expert mason and bricklayer, and after the Great Fire, his skills were in great demand in order to rebuild the city out of new bricks instead of wood. It is possible that most of the bricks he used to build his unusual-for-the-area Italianate-style home were salvaged from the destroyed buildings downtown. The home has foot-thick walls that have stood the test of time and will continue to do so.

Pietsch and his sons helped build several prominent buildings in Spokane, including the Great Northern Depot (now the clock tower) and the ever grand and gallant Davenport Hotel.

The Peaceful Valley area of Spokane was once known as Poverty Flats. Over the years, the neighborhood catered to the lower working class on the south bank of the river. After the 1889 fire, many immigrants moved into inexpensive, small houses in the narrow strip of land that was just down from Browne's Addition.

But the neighborhood was in need of a change, so in 1890 C.F. Clough (Spokane's mayor) platted the area into small lots and changed the name from the unsavory Poverty Flats to Peaceful Valley—and the sales soared. Pietsch was one of the first purchasers of the newly plotted sections of land, buying two lots for $550. Discovering the lots were of value, he soon bought a few more parcels and later a few more cottages to be used as rentals.

But this neighborhood took a turn toward the eerie side when in 1893 the Pietsch men unknowingly uncovered some ghastly remains. The Pietsch family was well known by locals for having an extensive and productive garden, which, of course, required a great deal of water. In order to obtain that water, they required access to a nearby spring. The

The Great Northern Railway depot and clock tower are backlit by the afternoon sun, taken somewhere between 1900 and 1920. *Spokane Public Library, photographer Frank Palmer.*

men quickly began digging a trench, eager to gain access to their much-needed water. But soon the pregnant wife of a next-door neighbor, Mrs. Haynes, walked over to the men and became very agitated by their digging and demanded they stop immediately. They were already tired, so without much argument, the men halted their work for the day.

The next morning, the Pietsch men resumed their digging with the help of a friend. After a few hours, an angry Mr. Haynes came over and confronted the men and demanded they stop digging. The Pietsch men advised Haynes that they had full permission to dig the trench and were not doing anything unlawful. Frustrated, Mr. Haynes returned to his house and retrieved his wife, who also confronted the men and demanded they stop digging at once. A mild fight began between the parties. The woman was focused on not digging in one particular section of the ditch, but the men refused to appease the angry woman and her unwarranted demand. The Haynes decided to go into town to try to get help from locals to make the men stop their digging.

Finally alone, the men shook their heads and resumed digging. As they dug the twenty-foot ditch to divert the water they needed to their garden, their shovels hit a few unexpected things—a skull and some human bones.

The men put the bones and skull in a bucket and took them to the Pietsch house to look at them more closely and contacted the local police. It was determined that the skull was that of a white male and he had been buried some four or five years prior.

The police questioned nearby neighbors, asking if any men had gone missing a few years earlier. Pietsch remembered a man that went by the name of Murphy who owned a garden lot here. Murphy reportedly sold his garden lot to Haynes (who had previously worked for him) and then made his way back to Canada.

But it was discovered that Murphy never went to Canada. Nor was he was ever heard from again.

Was the skull found that of Murphy? Did Haynes kill his prior employer for some unknown reason and bury his body in his garden? For some reason there was no follow-up investigation to determine the murderer or the identity of the victim.

Is Murphy the ghost who haunts the area?

Regardless of the skull and bones found in the nearby garden, the lovely home was enjoyed by Franz Pietsch and his family from 1891 until 1914; then other family members lived in it until 1929. From 1929 until 1960, it remained vacant or was used as a rental and sadly began to deteriorate—this is also when the ghostly sightings began. In 1997, the home was finally added to the National Register of Historic Places, and in 2003 it was purchased and slowly but surely renovated and returned to its original glory.

The brick Pietsch house will always remain a standing testament to the hardworking class of people who chased their dreams and built a wonderful life for themselves in the Peaceful Valley of Spokane.

NOTE: The Pietsch House is now a private residence being lovingly restored; please do not disturb the owner or nearby gardens.

3
HAUNTED HOTELS

"I think people see ghosts all the time," says Feng. "And I think ghosts want to be seen. They want to be reassured that they truly exist. They back into this world after passing through the gates of death into another dimension, and suddenly they hear every thought, speak every language, understand things they didn't get when they were alive."
—Emily X.R. Pan, The Astonishing Color of After

Spokane's wooden hotels had suffered fires and been rebuilt many times, like those of many other cities before the use of bricks for construction. After the 1889 fire, masons were in high demand, and some came from as far as Germany and Ireland to work in Spokane and start new lives.

After the horrific fire in 1889 that destroyed thirty-two city blocks, the first hotel to be built was the Merchant Hotel on west Riverside. Following suit, the Pacific, the Grand and the Hotel Spokane underwent extensive renovations. (They were not completely destroyed.)

Between 1907 and 1910, the city felt a big financial boom, which produced many more hotels, some seemingly trying to outdo one another in beauty and accommodations.

Although many still had common baths in the halls used by multiple rooms, the idea of private baths for each room was becoming more normal. Even the Davenport had only 370 baths for its 405 rooms.

The remains of the Great Eastern building from Riverside Avenue that burned on January 24, 1898, killing nine people. *Spokane Public Library.*

An unidentified group of men pose on a Spokane sidewalk alongside horse manure piles. The view is looking east from Stevens Street in 1895. *Washington State Archives.*

Unidentified men in 1885 working on construction on Riverside Avenue before the devastating fire of 1889. *Spokane Public Library.*

With many of the hotels destroyed and rebuilt, the residual energy that is retained can cause paranormal activity. Many stories of ghosts have been told over the years, and it seems as though spirits love to hang out in old hotels.

Unfortunately, many of the old hotels in Spokane were torn down and more modern buildings with both apartments and commercial spaces were built in their place. Do the ghosts haunt the new buildings, too? Unless more stories come forth, it is hard to tell.

Davenport Hotel

Two Ghosts Still Roam the Halls

A ghost story from W:
My uncle used to work at the Davenport Hotel, and he said strange things were always happening there. When I would try to get him to tell me what, he would shake his head and walk away. I think he was torn between not

A panoramic view of the haunted Davenport Hotel in downtown Spokane, 1896. *Library of Congress.*

believing in ghosts and having to deal with the reality that there are spirits that haunt certain places. I never did find out what he saw or heard while working there, but I do know he was affected by it. I don't think it was bad or scary, but it was definitely something he could not shrug off. I heard the man who built the Davenport haunts the place. I wish I knew for sure!

The Davenport Hotel takes the lead in Spokane's haunted history, along with the Patsy Clark mansion. The grand establishment at 807 West Sprague was designed by Llewellyn Marks "Louis" Davenport (1868–1951), who was also the proprietor. It is said to be haunted by two ghosts, but the most prominent is that of Mr. Davenport, who still roams the halls at 3:00 a.m. to check on guests and make sure *his* hotel is running smoothly. It is believed his spirit still resides in his old room, no. 1105, where he and his wife lived until both their deaths.

The other spirit is that of Ellen O'Donovan McNamara (1852–1920), who plunged to her death from the skylights at age sixty-eight. The story goes Ellen was traveling with her cousins and they were having dinner together when Ellen complained she wasn't feeling well. She excused herself and said she needed some fresh air…and that was her last breath.

Was it suicide? Murder? The world will never know, but her ghost continues to haunt the hotel to this day.

The Davenport family moved from New York to California in the mid-1800s, when Louis was just seven years old. As a teenager, Louis moved to Spokane in March 1889 and began working at the Pride of Seattle restaurant, located on Howard Street near the corner of Riverside (later destroyed by a fire).

It is reported that Davenport came to Spokane with a mere $1.50 in his pocket and later became listed as one of Spokane's millionaires (another rags-to-riches story!). He began his career in Spokane with the idea of a waffle stand after the fire in 1889, and thus began the Davenport Waffle Foundry, which consisted of just two tents and some used furniture, really. The devastating fire would not break Davenport's business sense or spirit down, although it did destroy virtually the entire city. This mindset is what eventually made Davenport one of the richest men in Spokane.

Davenport was interviewed about the aftermath and the quick rebuilding of businesses in tents on January 1, 1903, in the *Spokesman-Review*:

> *The day after the fire a large part of the population of Spokane took to cotton duck. Tents were pitched on every vacant lot....The hotel proprietors were hard put to accommodate their regular guests, to say nothing of the*

The haunted and incredibly enchanting Davenport Hotel as seen today from the street. *Author's collection.*

Spokane businesses refused to crumble after the fires and horrific devastation. People immediately began working from tents and partial buildings. *Spokane Public Library.*

Scene of Post Street looking south from Sprague Avenue showing Hazelwood Dairy and Mr. Davenport's first restaurant, taken somewhere between 1890 and 1900. *Spokane Public Library, Becher Collection, NWR.*

multitude of homeless men and women turned adrift by the disaster. Scores of hotels and lodging houses were set up under canvas. Some of these came to be very imposing affairs. Good accommodations in these canvas hotels cost from fifty cents to two dollars a night.

But Davenport had a keen sense for hospitality and a charismatic personality—one that would eventually make his mark on Spokane's history and eventually make him one of Spokane's listed millionaires. The majority of the funding for the new Davenport Hotel came primarily from two wealthy and influential men: William H. Cowles (1866–1946, the mulimillionaire newspaperman) and the famous James Hill (1838–1916, the Great Northern Railroad tycoon). Hearing of Davenport's incredible aptitude for hospitality and perfection, they offered to make him manager of the hotel. Having a keen sense of business, Davenport sold his home on Eighth Avenue to invest what he could in his next personal adventure—the incredible Davenport Hotel. At that time, he became just *one* of the other one hundred investors in the Davenport Hotel, but that didn't get him down.

He began helping create the Davenport Hotel by working with the famous local architect Kirtland Cutter. It would be located in the Wilson Block (where the hotel is currently located). In 1914, the construction cost

Right: A rare photograph of Louis Davenport, who *still* checks on his guests and hotel at 3:00 a.m. every night as reported by guests and staff. *NW Museum of Arts & Culture, purchased by Author.*

Below: Inside the extravagant Davenport Hotel with hand-painted murals, indoor garden trellises and lush greenery. *Washington State Archives.*

$1.75 million. Some of the big expenses were $85,000 worth of plasterwork, $50,000 in marble and $25,000 in tile. Per Cutter, the hotel was to have "Florentine detailing and Sullivanesque influences." The extravagant hotel was to become the tallest building in Spokane at the time.

It is hard to imagine just how extravagant the hotel was. It is no wonder spirits do not want to leave such a grand and amazing building. Some of the features (considered extremely over-the-top and lavish in that era) were a tennis court over the west wing, a hardball court over the east penthouse, formal indoor gardens with marble statues and fountains and Italian marble floors. From the start, and over the first few years, there were additions such as a barbershop, pharmacy, flower shop, Blue Bird Gift shop, piano retail store and soda fountain room. With the extravagant interiors of the Davenport Hotel, it is no wonder Louis's and his wife's spirits wish to never leave it.

The second floor of the hotel had a couple fascinating sections. One of the more interesting suites was the Isabella Room named in honor of Queen Isabella of Spain. The dining hall and ballroom boasted eight columns and extensive mirrors. Quaint figurines of rabbits, foxes, children and turtles adorned the room.

The two-story Marie Antoinette Room was styled in an eighteenth-century France influence with plaster court jesters and a magnificent ballroom with a suspended floor that would *move* with the dancers. The Elizabethan Room offered dark oak paneling with crests and gold leaf doors signifying a Tudor influence. The State Suite was reserved for powerful and notorious people like presidents, senators, governors, movie stars and tycoons.

But one of the strangest rooms was the Circus Room. It was designed in 1935 for a favorite guest and personal friend of Mr. Davenport's named Harper Joy who worked for the Ringling Brothers Circus as a clown (clowns are always creepy). Room no. 730 was decorated to make Joy feel at home when he stayed at the Davenport. Hand-painted murals depicting a circus parade were on the walls, and special light fixtures that looked like balloons added a final touch.

Over the years, as the hotel increased in popularity, the building underwent more transformations. In 1917, fifty-three more rooms were added. In 1929, an eleven-story, $240,000 addition on the south side was built, offering another eighty rooms.

The grand ballroom was quaintly called the "Hall of Doges," which translates to "Very Important." Much to the guests' delight, dancing promptly began at 9:00 p.m. nightly and went on until 1:00 a.m.

Opposite, top: With the extravagant interiors of the Davenport Hotel, it is no wonder both Louis and his wife's spirits do not wish to ever leave. *Washington State Archives, Libby Collection.*

Opposite, bottom: Many unidentified guests enjoy a luncheon at the Davenport Hotel in 1908, before McNamara's untimely fall to her death at the hotel. *Washington State Archives, Libby Collection.*

Above: A grand banquet given in the Davenport Hall of Doges in the Davenport Hotel in 1908. *Charles Libby Collection, Washington State Archives, Digital Archives.*

During construction, the hotel used a whopping thirty-two million pounds of steel and towered 157 feet into the air. At the time, it was the tallest building in Spokane.

Davenport was notorious for making sure that the luxurious wood-burning fireplace in the lobby was never left to burn out. Some say he still roams the hotel, making sure everything is in proper working order and that every detail is taken care of.

Although it seems that Davenport and McNamara notoriously haunt the hotel—there could be several other spirits that roam the halls, as many celebrities were fond of staying at the Davenport. Popular and famous guests included big names such as Bing Crosby, Amelia Earhart, Babe Ruth and

The Davenport lobby, where the ghost of Louis Davenport can often be seen. He loved to keep the fireplace burning day and night all year long. *Author's collection.*

Bob Barker as well as many U.S. presidents: Theodore Roosevelt, William Taft, Warren Harding, Harry Truman, John F. Kennedy, Lyndon Johnson and Richard Nixon.

In 1928, Davenport bought out many of the other investors of the hotel, making it his pride and joy for many years to come. He would often say he wanted his guests to "be glad they came, sorry to leave, and eager to return!"

But after fifty years of running the Davenport, Louis finally retired in 1945. He sold the hotel to the William Edris Company of Seattle for $1.5 million. Louis and his spouse, Verus E. Smith Davenport (1878–1967), remained living in room no. 1105 on the eleventh floor even after the sale. Louis died in the room in 1951, and Verus died in the same room sixteen years later.

When contractors were working on remodeling the room, they experienced objects moving, electrical issues and eerie feelings—could it be the ghosts of the Davenports not wanting their private room to be changed? Possibly.

The Davenport Hotel sadly closed in 1985 after it became run down. Luckily, a couple named Walt and Karen Worthy purchased the Davenport

The extravagant and luxurious Italian Room in the Davenport restaurant, 1908. *Charles Libby Collection, Washington State Digital Archives.*

in 2002, and it is now considered one of Spokane's top places to stay. It has been completely renovated from "top to bottom" and is proudly considered the greenest and most energy-efficient hotel in Washington. Louis would be proud indeed!

Louis Davenport may have died in 1951, but he left the Davenport and his name as an eternal Spokane legend. It is rumored he once told a concierge, "I never, ever want to leave my hotel." Perhaps Mr. Davenport is carrying out his wish and his ghostly spirit will continue to enjoy his glorious and enchanting hotel forever.

But what about the woman who fell to her death from the skylights on August 17, 1920, and is reportedly also haunting the hotel?

Ellen McNamara was a widow traveling with her sister and two cousins. On that fateful night, Ellen wasn't feeling well and decided to take in some fresh air. She walked toward the double doors that led out to the outside area and, moving through them, immediately felt the fresh air. She continued to walk around and, for some unknown reason, walked onto the catwalk for

Many mysterious and possibly symbolic ram heads adorn the Davenport Hotel's exterior. What do they symbolize? *Author's collection.*

workers and onto the glass ceiling, which promptly broke, and she fell to the marble floor below in the lobby. Much to the fear of the other hundred guests, the poor woman lay there in a pool of her blood as people tended to her. Dr. John O'Shea examined Ellen, but she died in her room later that evening. It is said her final words were, "Where did I go?"

The faint apparition of an elderly woman dressed in 1920s clothing has been seen walking around the lobby on the Davenport. The Spokane Ghost Crew captured on the EVP monitor the words *please, rescue, weeps* and *contrition*. Did Ellen walk on the glass on purpose? Was she sick or depressed? Was it suicide, or was someone else on the roof area that night who may have pushed her? Or was it as simple as a woman who wasn't feeling well who got disoriented and accidentally stepped on the glass and fell to her death? Since her demise, the hotel has installed a railing around the roof area and also installed a second glass roof over the original one for safety.

Ellen's restless spirit is obviously still wondering where she went when she died…hopefully someday her soul can move on to a peaceful place and she can rest silently.

NOTES:

A beautiful and fascinating pictorial compilation of photographs taken from the same spot every week from April 2 through December 10, 1913, shows the impressive construction of the Davenport Hotel, presented by the Spokane Historical Preservation Office. Go to: http://www.historicspokane.org/davenport.

Watch it—you will be glad you did!

An amazing and detailed collection of photographs of the Davenport Hotel can be found at the Charles Libby Collection online through the Northwest Museum of Arts and Culture at https://ferrisarchives.northwestmuseum.org.

A complete list of some of the other famous guests who have stayed in the glorious Davenport Hotel (and who may or may not be haunting their favorite hotel if they have already passed from this earthly world) are (from the hotel's website): Charles Lindbergh, Amelia Earhart, Mary Pickford, Clark Gable, John Philip Sousa, Lawrence Welk, Bob Hope, Bing Crosby, Benny Goodman, Vachel Lindsay, John F. Kennedy, Babe Ruth, Vicki Lawrence, Cuba Gooding Jr., Angie Harmon, James Woods, Burt Reynolds, Josh Hartnett, James Spader, Henry Winkler, Ray Allen, Kristi

Yamaguchi, Michelle Kwan, Dennis Franz, Huey Lewis and the News, Sandra Day O'Connor, Salma Hayek, Jessica Biel, Samuel L Jackson, 50 Cent, Debbie Reynolds, Wayne Newton, Christina Ricci, John Travolta, Harry Connick Jr., Kevin Durant, Keith Urban, Newt Gingrich, Snoop Dogg, Tony Bennett, Jay Leno, Howie Mandel, Neil Sedaka, Bob Newhart, Carrie Underwood, BB King, Ringo Starr, Michael McDonald Charro, Cheech and Chong, Regis Philbin, k.d. lang, Dick Cheney, Don Rickles, Bernadette Peters, Taylor Swift, Jay Mohr, Pat Benatar, Demi Moore, David Duchovny, Lyle Lovett, Peter Frampton, John Tesh, Wynonna Judd, Dionne Warwick, Michael Bolton, Bryan Adams, Cheap Trick, Neil Everett, Antonio Banderas, Melanie Griffith, Ed Asner, Natalie Cole, Conan O'Brien, Doobie Brothers, Zig Ziglar, Travis Tritt, Dane Cook, Sarah McLaughlin, Yanni, Rod Stewart, Andy Garcia, Tony Hawk, Jim Gaffigan, Bonnie Raitt, Tracy Morgan, LeAnn Rimes, Sarah Palin, Fleetwood Mac, Russell Wilson, Dennis Miller, Jay Bilas, Dana Carvey, Kid Rock and Meredith Vieira.

RIDPATH HOTEL

A Hotel with a Fascinating Past

The Ridpath Hotel located at 515 West Sprague is one of Spokane's most interesting buildings, as it is as rich in history as it is in drama. Although few rumors of hauntings exist (yet several YouTube videos from paranormal investigators claim it is haunted by former tenants or soiled doves from the past who will move money left on nightstands), the building itself is worth a mention because of its wonderful part in Spokane's history.

Some of that history is both funny and interesting, such as rumors of Evil Kneivel (1938–2007, a famous motorcycle stuntman) and his friend getting into a fight over a former lover, some sort of drug trafficking, various lawsuits, fires, a stolen $25,000 Steinway grand piano, fraud accusations, part of a movie production (*Vision Quest*, 1985), financial troubles and looming foreclosures, expensive renovations—along with positive aspects like the fact that famous celebrities such as Michael Jackson (1958–2009) and Elvis Presley (1935–1977) enjoyed staying there and the hotel ran continuously for 108 years.

In 1973, Elvis came to perform a concert in Spokane and rented fifty-five hotel rooms on three of the floors for his managers, musician, friends

The somewhat haunted Ridpath hotel on West Sprague Street is a landmark for Spokane. *Author's collection.*

and clan. Elvis also stayed at the Ridpath Hotel in 1957 during a concert. Obviously, Elvis loved staying at the Ridpath Hotel.

Fascinating history aside, the Ridpath Hotel remains a Spokane icon and hopefully will continue to grace the city with its presence. Perhaps the ghost of Elvis or Michael is haunting the hotel? The two former musical kings would certainly be welcome. Or it is the spirit of Colonel Ridpath himself who haunts the massive hotel that he built, proud of his accomplishment?

The hotel is now actually two buildings: the high-rise, thirteen-floor tower built in 1952 (called "The Tower") and the original four-story brick building from 1905 (the "east Wing"). The 1952 hotel replaced the two previous Ridpath Hotels.

The first and original Ridpath Hotel was built as a first-class accommodation in 1899 and opened in 1900. Unfortunately, it was destroyed

A rare photograph of Colonel Ridpath, who built the beautiful Ridpath Hotel. *From the* Newport Miner, *August 8, 1912.*

in a fire in 1903 but rebuilt. An ad in the *Spokane City Directory* boasted it had "100 daylight rooms and 50 private baths!"

Colonel William Marion Ridpath (1845–1914) was born in Indiana and enlisted at the age of seventeen years as a Union soldier in Company H, 115th Indiana Infantry. After he studied law for years, he was admitted to the bar in 1872. In 1882, he was appointed the Indian agent for the Yankton Sioux of South Dakota. He married Sarah Jane Cole (1851–1922), and they had four children. In 1888, the Ridpath family moved to Spokane, where he practiced law for twelve years. He then invested in the LeRoy mine and made a small fortune, which he promptly put into the creation of his Ridpath Hotel. The *Spokane Press* advertised it on October 10, 1903: "The hotels proprietress was Mrs. E. Eaton and the hotel was a 3-story brick building with 200 feet of frontage. It had 100 daylight rooms with private baths that rented for $1 to $3 per day."

The hotel unfortunately suffered from a fire on December 12, 1902, and although the guests got away in their nightclothes, the building was not so lucky. The fire started in the basement, reportedly by the night baker. The loss was estimated at $200,000 (approximately worth $5,981,581 at the inflation rate today).

The hotel was rebuilt and continued to run smoothly until 1913, when Colonel Ridpath was arrested for an unusual thing. The *Lynden Tribune* reported that "Ridpath was arrested for failure to supply his beds with sheets 81" wide by 90" long!" Imagine that.

Sheet "rules" were apparently a big thing in Spokane during the early 1900s during the overflow of workers with nowhere to lodge. Many buildings housed dozens of men sleeping on dirt floors or in chairs. As noted in 1909, the proprietor of the New York house was "fined $10 for violating the hotel sheet law by using only one sheet per bed instead of two."

Ridpath died in 1914, and the Ridpath family owned and ran the hotel until 1988, when it was sold.

One guest that stayed at the Ridpath and unfortunately died there was Harry Green (1863–1910). He died on December 7, 1910, of Bright's disease at the hotel. His ghost might be lingering in the halls. Green was responsible for giving Spokane the best baseball team, was a brilliant prize fight manager and did more to develop Spokane's sports than any other man at the time. He was also the half owner and proprietor of Spokane's Club Café. Green was lovingly nicknamed the "Duke of Spokane."

But the Ridpath was in for more trouble. Another fire broke out in 1950 that completely destroyed the original building. On February 28, a massive fire burned for thirteen hours straight and did $1 million damage to the five-story hotel. The building was unsalvageable.

It was rebuilt on the same location and reopened in 1952 as the Ridpath Tower, a twelve-story 130-foot-high, 250-room hotel. It cost $3 million to build and was considered the top hotel in Spokane's downtown district. It had views from every room, underground parking for one hundred cars (a new Spokane feature) and commercial spaces on the main floor. It also had the new idea of a drive-in lobby (the only one in the West), which went over very well. When all was said and done, the new Ridpath also included interior furnishings that cost $450,000.

Other fascinating features were its Oval Terrace and King Cole dining room and lounge. The Ridpath Tower was touted as one of the finest hotels in Spokane and had the first and only "all-welded steel frame multi-story high-rise hotel building constructed west of the Mississippi River." It contained over nine hundred tons of steel.

The Ridpath is being renovated and will continue to be a part of Spokane's wonderful history.

DOUBLETREE HOTEL/MIRABEAU PARK HOTEL

Some Ghosts Never Check Out

More than one ghost haunts the hotel at 1100 North Sullivan Road in Spokane. (It has changed names and owners several times over the years.) Many reports of a female ghost with her two small children walk the halls and cause chaos and mischief. Another male entity who supposedly committed suicide near the front desk still roams the hotels halls. On the third floor, a very friendly ghost continually asks the hotels staff for fresh towels.

Who are these spirits, and why do they haunt the hotel? Unless some paranormal researchers get some hard evidence, all we have are stories of objects moving, strange phone calls, some apparitions…but no hard evidence or documentation. Multiple websites just say the same few paragraphs over and over. Who is the man who committed suicide? Who is the woman and her two children? Why does the towel ghost keep seeking fresh linens?

Perhaps someday the ghosts at Mirabeau Park Hotel will come forward long enough to share their stories. Until then, the hotel will continue to offer great accommodations and friendly service to all guests—living or not.

RUBY HOTEL

A WWI Hospital Called Lion Hotel

In 1918, the Ruby Hotel was called the Lion Hotel, and it was located on the corner of South Lincoln and West First Avenue near the Deaconess Hospital (also reported to be haunted). It was turned into a makeshift hospital during World War I when the Spanish flu epidemic hit hard, killing over five hundred Spokane residents in one year. The Red Cross, running out of room at its hospitals and other spaces, demanded the city establish another temporary location to house infected people, possibly one of its hotels. They decided on the Lion Hotel due to its location. All patients had to pay ten dollars up front to be held there. The manager of the Lion at the time agreed to heat the hotel and provide fresh linens for the patients. When it was used as a temporary influenza hospital, hundreds of people died in that building. The final death count is unclear.

The Spanish flu also affected over 175,000 soldiers during this time of war. The Spanish flu infects the lungs and then quickly turns into pneumonia. Boston got hit the hardest, with over 30,000 cases in the city.

With the coronavirus today, it is not so hard to see how it affected the community profusely. Churches and theaters had to space out individuals, spanning them between every other pew or section; plus they had to shut down every night to ventilate the building. Retail stores were not allowed to advertise any special sales for the fear of bringing a group of shoppers together in one place. Public schools could only be open if they offered one thousand cubic feet of air space for each student.

Spokane got hit with over 11,000 cases of the Spanish flu in one year, and 562 citizens died. It is no wonder that the old hotel is rumored to be haunted. Current patrons and employees reported that the bar is the most haunted hot spot in the building.

For over 140 years, there has been a hotel at 901 West First Avenue, and the accommodations continue today, offering incredible lodgings, service and entertainment to all who enter its doors.

The Deaconess Hospital is located at 800 West Fifth Avenue, and a phantom ghost continues to reside in the northern elevator. Rumor suggests a former worker named Charlie was killed by the elevator when it malfunctioned. Established in 1896, it was the first hospital in Spokane. The hospital is now an award-winning facility that offers many services to local residents. Perhaps the ghost of Charlie is still enjoying helping to run the elevators for the many patients and employees?

4

HAUNTED HOT SPOTS

The popular notion that ghosts are likely to be seen in a graveyard is not borne out by psychical research….A haunting ghost usually haunts a place that a person lived in or frequented while alive….Only a gravedigger's ghost would be likely to haunt a graveyard.
—John Alexander, Ghosts! Washington Revisited: The Ghostlore of the Nation's Capitol

MARKET STREET ANTIQUES

Voices from the Past

A day will come when certain antiques and old homes will be able to play sounds and voices of our past like record players. Technology will scan the grooves embedded within them as mediums can do without it.
—Lorin Morgan-Richards

A ghost story from Mark Porter of Spokane Paranormal Society:
Whenever we investigate Market Street Antiques, we communicate with same two male entities—both of which have a sense of humor. They are both older men. The names they provide are "Walter" and "Willy." Walter died of cancer and likes to flirt with the ladies. He loves to be in the shop. Willy is a railroad switchman who liked to have a drink now and then and who is also very friendly. There are no negative spirits in the store.

The building located at 4912 North Market Street in the Hillyard neighborhood offers more than just an incredible selection of antiques. The two-story location has over twenty-five vendors who specialize in Native American collectible antiques, vintage kitchen cabinets and furniture items and just about anything else you might want. With this huge array of old items, it is possible that the spirits who haunt the building might be clinging to their favorite furniture or simply feel more comfortable around old things. The building was also a furniture store in 1903, and it is also the oldest building in the Hillyard historic district. Then in 1919, it was home to the *Inland Empire News*. In 1984, it was the site of the Cloak and Dagger Antiques. The new owner, Susan Hess, acquired the building in 2002.

Some of the paranormal activity noted includes apparitions of a family and toys or small objects moving on their own. Paranormal psychics and researchers believe that there is a female spirit in her mid-thirties who likes to peer out the windows. What is she searching for? The psychics also revealed another ghost that roams the building is a male in his fifties who wears overalls. He is believed to be a switchman named John Olson who died in 1939 at the age of forty-nine.

Research by the author reveals that there actually was a man named John Olson who worked for the Great Northern Railroad as a switchman of a fruit train in Hillyard. He tragically died one day in a train accident near the haunted site, sadly leaving his wife and five children behind. Did he also go by the nickname Willy?

The "Hill"yard area became a township around 1892, when the great railroad mastermind James Hill brought his Great Northern railway to the towns to expand his hub for the Inland Empire region. Soon other railroad companies followed suit, making Spokane one of the biggest transportation centers in Washington. Most of the homes built were to house workers of the railroad and are still intact.

The Hillyard business district on Market Street today is the first neighborhood in Spokane to be listed in the National Register of Historic Places, as it retains the most collective original architecture from almost one hundred years ago. One can truly experience a trip back in time when visiting Hillyard and perhaps see a ghost or two from its interesting past.

Sometimes a sudden, accidental death can cause the spirit to remain in the location until they choose to move on in the spirit world. Is that the case for the switchman who lingers at the antique store where he once worked for the railroad until his tragic death?

Drumheller Springs

A Cattle Rustler and Indian Fight

The legend of Dan Drumheller (1840–1925) and an unnamed Spokane Indian has been buried a long time. The truth of the matter is still a mystery, as the real murderer's identity was never discovered.

The story begins a long time ago in March 1910, when Drumheller, who ran a large cattle slaughterhouse near the springs, was running a group of sheep across a bridge (located on the north section of Howard Street) and into town. It was said he built the slaughterhouse at that site not only for the availability of fresh water but also to keep the railroad from running through the area. Supposedly, an intoxicated Indian was trying to scare Drumheller's sheep as he approached. The men began to argue, and it came out that the Indian had indeed been drinking. Drumheller reportedly hit him with a stick. Deputy M. Gillian broke up the confrontation and dragged the Indian to the local jail to sleep it off for the night.

Sometime in the dark hours, an unknown assailant snuck up to the jail, peered through the bars and shot the Indian in cold blood. The Indian died later on Friday night. Drumheller claimed he was innocent of the murder.

Another story goes that Drumheller was running his livestock through town—in this story it was cattle—and was approached by a hostile Indian. City marshal E.B. Hyde was called. Supposedly, Drumheller urged his large group of cattle onward and ran over the Indian, who later died.

Drumheller was charged with the murder, but the jury acquitted him. Was Drumheller guilty? Did the jury look the other way because his victim was an Indian? The truth may never really be known.

It was well known that Drumheller (originally from Tennessee, he had trekked from Missouri to California on a wagon train in 1854) had a good reputation as an upstanding and productive Spokane citizen. It is written in newspapers that he was one of the city's earliest pioneers, had remarkable judgment, was quick-witted and honorable. He ran the Big Bend National Bank, was the mayor of Spokane in 1891, had earlier ran on the Pony Express and even survived contracting Rocky Mountain spotted fever. He and his large family lived at 1321 Sixth Avenue in Spokane, and he was known locally as "Uncle Dan." At one time, he had over fourteen thousand cattle in various parts of the country.

In 1860, Drumheller participated in the Pyramid Lake Indian War (also called the Paiute War) that took place in Utah Territory (now Nevada), where eighty white men were killed. The battle was an ugly one between the Washoe Indian tribe and white settlers. Since he partook in the conflict, was he prejudiced against Indians?

NOTE: After research, I discovered that Drumheller had good relations with the Indians and even gave them all of the "parts" of the slaughtered cattle that the white customers would not eat. The Indians did not waste anything, and they greatly appreciated Drumheller's scraps. Some Indians even waited daily by his business in order to collect the meat to disperse to the tribe. So animosity between the Indians and Drumheller does not seem likely to the author.

When the area is investigated by paranormal researchers, they pick up on "rivers of blood," which are probably from the cleaning up of the cattle slaughterhouse. They also pick up on the anger and frustrations from the Indians that used to reside there, as it was their native lands and the white settlers did run them off. It is reported that the area was a well-known burial site for the local Indians, so this would have caused some ill feelings between the Indians and white settlers. It may also account for any paranormal activity in the area if the graves were disturbed.

The Dan Drumheller Springs (also called Lone Pine) area is known for its steep slopes and unusual land that was formed from glacial activity and the Missoula Flood (at the end of the last Ice Age).

The area was also a gathering and trading site for the local tribes and a popular water source for everyone from Indians to fur traders to soldiers and miners. At the time, it was the *only* available source for fresh water on North Hill.

A great man named Chief Spokane Garry (also spelled Spokan and Gary, 1811–1892) ran a school there in the 1800s for sixty years where he taught religion and farming to the locals. Chief Garry started exploration at the young age of fourteen in 1825. He quickly learned both the English and French languages along with agricultural skills. Chief Garry built a small church and gathering place with the help of the local tribes. His reed mat church was a spot where all could gather to learn English and Christianity.

NOTE: There is a wooden marker honoring Chief Garry on Ash Street toward Fairview Ave on the north side. Today, the area enjoys a more peaceful environment. The Eastern Washington Historical Society purchased part of the land to create a recreational area. Local schoolchildren can visit the twelve-acre Dan Drumheller Park and enjoy learning about nature and wildlife.

Although no known hauntings come from this next story, another local man who was of significant importance to teaching the children of the Spokane tribes was Reverend Henry T. Cowley and his wife, Abigail. They were one of the four first settlers to the Spokane Falls area in 1874. Although none of the original buildings remain, Cowley built a small log cabin on the land with the help of the local Indians. The land was part of the area ran by a subchief of Spokane known as Enoch. The Indians helped Cowley build the home in exchange for a horse and a significant amount of grain. Cowley built the first public school and had six students in attendance. There he lovingly and patiently taught the local children of the tribes to speak English. A park has been dedicated to the Cowleys in honor of all their hard work and devotion to Spokane and the relationships they created with the local tribes. It is located at 602 South Division between Sixth and Seventh Avenues in the Cliff/Cannon neighborhood.

The Mysterious Painted Rocks

A story from Carla from Washington:
I heard about the hand-painted rocks the local Indians drew on a cliff in a park in Spokane. Being an artist myself, I make it a mission to check these things out. We arrived at the park and walked to the fenced area where the rock paintings are. I took pictures with my camera to analyze later. I could clearly make out a horse, a cross, circles and maybe what could be cabins? As we were looking at the paintings, I felt a great sense of peace and serenity. Maybe it was just because it was a beautiful sunny day (rare in Washington), but I don't think so. The feeling seemed to come from inside *my chest area. One way to explain it is it felt like my heart was* enlarging....*Since I did not think it was of medical urgency (I have no history of heart illness or problems), I decided to meditate on this feeling and see where it took me. I closed my eyes and just let my mind drift. I knew my pals wouldn't care, as they are very spiritual as well.*

After a few minutes of meditation, I saw in my mind's eye a young Indian as he was staring at the rock. Call me crazy, but I am just telling you what I saw in my mind. Some friends think I am sorta psychic. Anyway, I could clearly see this young man staring at the rock, like he was visualizing his artistic expression and pondering what he might want to paint. He was grinding something with a rock in like a stone bowl not much bigger than his hand. I watched him as he slowly made his paintings, one "stroke" at a time (he had to keep dipping his rock into the other rock). It made me feel such a magnificent sense of connection with this fellow artist! To think in my mind I could actually watch this man create his beautiful paintings in my head! Again, call me crazy…

It went on for a just a few minutes, then I opened my eyes. My friends were staring at me. I said, "What?" They said, "Who were you talking to?" I said, "No one. I was just meditating." They smiled and said, "Uhm, no, you were talking to someone, like in some weird language."

I was a little shocked. I don't remember talking at all. I did my ancestry thing once and it said I have some Native American blood in me. After they said this, I wondered if maybe I had known this man in a past life or something? Why would I be talking to him in a weird language? Now I wish they would have recorded me so I could see a university or someone could translate it!

One other gorgeous and mysterious area for Spokane is the incredible and rare hand-painted rocks found by a fur trader, created over two hundred years ago by an unknown Indian artist. The "paint" for the cryptic artwork was made by crushing red stones and mixing them with fish oil. This paint was then administered to the flatter portions of the large rock to make the art. The color permeated the larger stones' surface and became permanent. Did the artist somehow know this would last for hundreds of years? Was it a process other Indians had passed down over the generations? The artist may have been a member of the early Salishan tribe. It is thought that the inland northwest area was used by local Indians for thousands of years prior to white settlers moving into the territory.

Researchers believe that the art reveals such things as hunting and fishing records, religious thoughts or simply art. These Indian pictographs clearly show a cross and a horse. There are Water Devil designs on the right side, which are known to symbolize that there are bad spirits nearby. Maybe a written warning to others passing by?

There are two groups of paintings: the first being a six-foot-by-six-foot area on a cliff that measures twenty by twenty-five feet. The second section measures approximately four feet by two and a half feet. The artwork was at one time painted over by a horribly rude and unknown assailant, but luckily, the artwork was salvaged and it is now protected by a fence. The historical significance of these paintings is rare because so many pictographs have been lost over the years to vandalism, river erosion and developments. The fact that these exist is a real treasure and treat, and hopefully no more destruction will occur and many generations to come can enjoy their beauty.

Maybe someday someone can decipher the paintings' meaning, but until then the art made by the unknown creator hundreds of years ago can only be treasured, protected and enjoyed.

NOTE: To see these wonderful paintings, visit 5694 West Rutter Parkway at the Little Spokane River Natural Area in the State Park off the St. George Trailhead.

Spokane Indians and Bigfoot

When the early white men began settling in the area of Spokan Falls, the local Indians already had a legend about large, hairy creatures that roamed the area. A missionary named Reverend Elkenah Walker (1805–1877) and his wife, Mary, traveled from Maine to Missouri on horseback and continued on to Walla Walla, then to the Oregon Territory after an urgent call for their services. Walker became an ordained minister in 1838.

They later came to the Spokane area from Fort Colville (after their friend and fellow traveler Doctor Whitman was killed) in the late 1840s, where they spent ten years among the Indians. Walker and Mary took a keen interest in the spoken language of the local tribe and patiently learned their language instead of forcing English on the natives. He wrote the only book ever written in their language.

There is evidence of a letter written by the Walkers concerning the existence of a large beast in the area. Walker strongly believed that the presence of a giant creature could be found at the top of a nearby mountain. These beasts came out only at night and were known to steal sleeping people and their food (mostly salmon). The victims would wake up bewildered and lost. The Indians told of the beasts' horrible, strong odor. They also remarked that the creatures communicated through a series of grunts, sounds and whistles. The creatures had incredible strength, and their tracks were over one and a half feet long. Sure sounds like Bigfoot!

Was this really Bigfoot or simply a larger-than-life group of men wearing buffalo hides and roaming the mountains? Since there were no cameras back then, the only evidence gathered was from stories and tales told and repeated around the campfire and passed down from the tribes.

MONAGHAN HALL AT GONZAGA

Phantom Music and Noises

A ghost story from a former student:
I haven't had to deal with any ghosts, but my friend experienced stuff when at Gonzaga. She would hear footsteps all the time when she was pretty sure the place was empty. The scariest was when she was just walking past the building one evening and she said all the hair on her arms and on her head felt like it was poking up and then she felt what seemed like someone's finger moving down her spine! It freaked her out really bad.

The music department on the campus of Gonzaga University in Monaghan Hall is a well-known and documented haunt. Stories of the furniture moving and piano or organ music being heard are very popular. Who is haunting the campus? The building was once the private residence of James Monaghan. False rumors and tales that Monaghan was murdered at the location persist but are completely untrue.

James Monaghan (1839–1916), who became one of Spokane's wealthiest men, was born in Ireland. He was orphaned at age three. At the young age of seventeen, he made his way to America in search of his dreams. Monaghan

A Gonzaga College building in 1910. The music hall is reported to be haunted, and there was even an exorcism performed there in the 1970s. *Washington State Archives.*

did fulfill his dreams, and by 1909 he was listed as one of Spokane's most prominent millionaires, earning him the nickname "Spokane Jim." Again, another rags-to-riches Spokane patron.

But his story was not of an easy life—he suffered financial losses during the Panic of 1893 and then two years later lost his beloved wife, Margaret, who died at just forty-two years old, leaving four young children behind. More tragedy was to strike later when his son John Robert (1873–1899) died while serving in the U.S. Navy at age twenty-six. Years earlier, young John attended Gonzaga College (as it was called back then) in 1887 and was part of the eighteen who graduated that year. After graduating, he served on the USS *Olympia* and was promoted to ensign (ranking above chief warrant officer 5 and directly below lieutenant junior grade) in 1897 on the gunboat USS *Alert*, operating on the West Coast. In 1898, he began serving during the Spanish-American War as officer on the USS *Philadelphia*, which was later sent to the Samoan Islands. Rebel Samoans were causing great troubles, and when Monaghan's unit leader, Lieutenant Philip Lansdale (1858–1899), was critically injured after being shot in the leg, Monaghan hurriedly went to his rescue.

Sadly, on April 1, John Monaghan was tragically killed in action during an ambush by the hostile Samoans at the First Battle of Vailele, Samoa. The official report of the action stated:

> *The men were not in sufficient numbers to hold out any longer, and they were forced along by a fire which it was impossible to withstand. Ensign Monaghan did stand. He stood steadfast by his wounded superior and friend—one rifle against many, one brave man against a score of savages. He knew he was doomed. He could not yield. He died in heroic performance of duty.*

The brave war hero, who died at such an early age, is honored by a statue erected in 1906 at the corner of North Monroe Street and Riverside Avenue. The inscription reads: "During the retreat of the allied forces from the deadly fire and overwhelming number of the savage foe, he alone stood the fearful onslaught and sacrificed his life defending a wounded comrade Lieutenant Philip V. Lansdale United States Navy." Two U.S. Navy ships—a destroyer in World War I and another in World War II—were also named after him.

Some believe it is John Monaghan who haunts the Gonzaga music hall because he associates the home with his family, not the hardship known to soldiers during the horrors of war. Although the mansion was built in 1898 and John never lived there, his spirit might be returning to where his family once lived peacefully and happily together for years, possibly to somehow partake in those moments.

John's father, James Monaghan, made his fortune in Spokane by running boats across the Coeur d'Alene River. He also founded the Saint Vincent DePaul Society in 1889. He was a well-respected and loved citizen of Spokane, and during one of the city's most horrible fires he helped feed hundreds of people.

In 1903, Monaghan bought the Eagle block at Stevens and Riverside Streets for $100,000. In 1909, he bought two lots at Main and Browne Streets to build a five-story building that cost him another $100,000. James was a good businessman, and everyone had great things to say about him and his family.

The haunted and stately mansion at 217 East Boone Avenue was built by architects Herman Preusse and Julius Zittel as a private residence in 1889 for Monaghan and his family. The giant wraparound curved porch, many columns, grand turret and arched windows are all part of a spectacular design that is both elegant and fascinating.

Monaghan peacefully died of natural causes in his bed at his mansion surrounded by his family in 1916. The hauntings do not seem to be related to James Monaghan in any way. The mansion was later purchased by the university in 1942. Some believe the mansion is haunted by his son John, as the beautiful home was linked to his family. Who wouldn't want to hang out in such a glorious mansion?

Others feel the place is haunted by a former college student who committed suicide in the attic. The paranormal activities in the building are reported as electrical failures for no reason, phantom footsteps when no one else is around, extreme cold spots, shadowy figures in windows, the smell of smoke and doors being unlocked when they were recently locked by security guards.

The most notorious and creepy activity is the sound of organ music when no one is near to play the instrument. It has been said that the music heard is the very same music that was played at James Monaghan's funeral! Several photos of the original owner of the mansion lying in his coffin have been found in the walls and basement of the building. Who hid them there and why?

An exorcism was performed in the building in 1975 by Father Walter Leedale (1923–2008) to quiet any restless and naughty spirits. A year earlier, many concerned students approached Leedale with their fears. They were complaining to him about cold spots, eerie music, phantom footsteps and much more—making their time spent at the music hall extremely frightening. Father Leedale, being a man of faith, wanted to put these worries and fears to rest once and for all for the sake of the university. He decided to stay the night in the office to prove to the students that there was nothing unusual going on.

But that was not the case…

He soon heard musical melodies and was perplexed because he *knew* he was the only person in the building at that time. After searching the rooms and finding no one, he truly began to wonder what was going on. One story involves Leedale reaching to open a door: the knob somehow turned itself, and the door opened.

He later approached a housekeeper and told her what had happened that night. She lit up and confessed that she too heard the music often when she was alone cleaning the building. She would follow the sound of the music to a locked practice room on the lower level where there was an organ. She found the organ playing by itself by invisible fingers. She knew the room was not occupied by anyone when she first heard the music— at least not anyone *living*.

To make matters worse, Leedale was disturbed by growling noises, and when he and a security officer followed the terrifying sound, it led to a locked door. When the security officer unlocked and opened the door, nothing but a broken cello and an axe were inside. Needless to say, the men were thoroughly puzzled and scared.

In late February, Leedale, two security men and Daniel Brenner of the music department all experienced bone-chilling paranormal activity that none of them could explain. Father Leedale knew he had to take immediate measures and precautions to protect the students and faculty members and anyone else who set foot in the mansion. He began a series of prayers for protection that continued for several days. During those frightful days, Leedale experienced what he considered negative paranormal activity, but he would not give up hope.

After his continued blessings and prayers, the negative energy seemed to leave the building, much to Leedale's relief. Several years before his death, Leedale told the *Pacific Northwest Inlander*, "Honest to God, I don't know what it was, but I can say that Christians believe there are evil forces in the world, and that we, as Christians, pray to God to protect us from them, or for the strength to deal with them. This is what I was doing at the music building."

Today, the university would like to think that any ghosts have moved on and the students can peacefully enjoy playing music without the interference of ghosts. It seems as though any negative energy was banished by Leedale's prayers and no more frightening growls or paranormal activities have been happening. The staff and students can relax and enjoy the beautiful campus and the mansion—as Mr. Monaghan would have loved if he were still alive.

But only time will tell.

GREENWOOD CEMETERY

The One Thousand Haunted Steps

A ghost story from Gill:
A long time ago, you could climb the steps there at the cemetery, not sure if you still can now with all that's going on in the world. But back then me and my buddies were up to this crazy challenge that spirits would somehow hold you back from reaching the top. Well, we felt brave that afternoon, so as a group (haha) we set out to accept the challenge. I don't know if it was our adrenaline or actual paranormal activity, but I did feel a weird tugging at my left arm about halfway up. That was all though. I did experience some very creepy stuff when we were walking through the cemetery. Now I wish I would have gone and seen what grave she was at, but I didn't think about it at the time. I didn't tell my buddies either although I should have. It was a bigger tombstone off to the right.

Anyway, I saw a woman kneeling down in front of one of the larger tombstones, and it looked like she had clothes from a long time ago on, like a really thick wool skirt. When I saw her, she looked over at me and just stared at me for a second or two. I remember thinking, Gosh, she looks so incredibly sad....I have never seen someone look so sad. And then she was gone! Another strange thing...don't think I am weird, but as I saw her I also had this overwhelming sense to comfort her somehow. I will never forget her eyes, the pain and sadness in them. It's like the pain she was feeling was oozing out of her eyes, like when someone has been crying for a really, really, really long time.

Of all the cemeteries in Washington, possibly Greenwood Cemetery is the most haunted of all. The most notorious tale of the paranormal has to do

The crumbling "1,000" haunted steps at the Greenwood Cemetery with the Elks mausoleum at the top of them. *Spokane Paranormal Society.*

with the cemetery's creepy and reportedly haunted "thousand" steps. In reality, there are only sixty-six, but while attempting to climb them all the way to the top they probably feel like one thousand. Ghostly spirits are said to prevent curious people from reaching the top of the crumbling stairs by "blocking" them. It is said that eerie sensations develop on your skin as you walk up the steps. Others claim they hear screams from the dead. Located at 211 North Government Way, the cemetery itself has an interesting part in Spokane's history—along with the accumulation of Spokane spirits.

Three ghosts of workmen who died in the tunnel are said to haunt the grounds as well as several prominent Spokane citizens such as Amasa Campbell, Anthony Cannon and James Glover. At the top of the stairs, there are still the remains of a once beautiful mausoleum, and in earlier times several Elks members wanted to eventually be entombed together there.

There was a track at the entrance where a trolley would drop visitors off up at the cemetery. This original entrance is still located where it was back then. Some believed there was a secret hidden tunnel that burrowed underground for rituals, but that idea probably stemmed from the old railroad tunnel that did exist.

More interesting is the history between the cemetery and the Spokane Elks Organization No. 228 (founded in 1892 with just forty-three members). In 1898, the Elks members agreed to purchase plots for themselves, their wives and children at the Greenwood Cemetery if the cemetery built the stairs, second terrace and fraternal mausoleum. By 1907, famed architect Kirkland Cutter and fellow designer Malmgren had conceived the beautiful mausoleum for the Elks. It included expensive bronze gates, a life-size bronze elk and a bronze clock (with the hands frozen at eleven o'clock—a tradition in honor of fellow Elks members that had died). As beautiful as the land and setup was, the plot layout was the death of the idea, as the men were going to be buried in the upper terrace and the wives and children in the lower part. The wives obviously became angry at this arrangement, and the whole premise was waylaid. The mausoleum remained empty even as members died off. Today it is used for nothing more than storage.

In the 1970s, the Elks began experiencing financial problems, and in 1981 they had to sell off their beloved elk statue to settle debts. (The elk statue was eventually returned to the cemetery and is now in a private place for safekeeping.) Only the bronze clock hands remain on the mausoleum, but they are no longer set at the eleventh hour.

One of the ghosts said to haunt the Greenwood Cemetery is Spokane pioneer Anthony McCue Cannon (1839–1895), also called the "Father

ANTHONY M. CANNON.

An ink illustration of Anthony Cannon, who was sometimes called the "Father of Spokane." *From the* Spokane Post Intelligencer, *April 7, 1895.*

of Spokane." In 1888, he desired to build a railroad to compete with Northern Pacific Railway on the property where the cemetery now exists. His railroad idea didn't fly. With the land in Spokane being in great demand, the old graves in the former pioneer cemeteries needed to be relocated. But where? Anthony Cannon and several other businessmen set out to solve this problem by purchasing land in order to build a new cemetery. Problem solved! Soon, over fifty graves were dug up, and the bodies exhumed were to be moved from the Old Mountain View Cemetery in Cannon's Addition on the lower South Hill to their new final resting place.

Cannon's spirit is believed to roam the cemetery for unknown reasons, and it is said he is the most prominent ghost. Some think it is because he is angry and jealous that the Great Northern Railroad (GNRR) succeeded in building a railway there—his original idea. Where did they build it? *Under the cemetery.* GNRR engineers reportedly (just to rub it in) would blow their train's whistle as they passed under the approximate area of Cannon's grave. How rude! That is enough to anger any ghost.

Anthony Cannon's life was quite fascinating. He was born to a very poor family in Illinois, and at age twenty he promptly left home and headed west in search of a better life for himself. He roamed such big cities as San Francisco, Chicago, Denver, Kansas City and Portland before coming to Spokane in 1878 on a horse. He lived in a modest wooden cabin located where the First Presbyterian Church stands today. Cannon quickly started buying land, and he and J.J. Browne together bought half of Glover's town sites.

He later started a bank and worked as Spokane's first banker, then became the city's second mayor. Cannon eventually became one of the richest men in Eastern Washington, with a net worth of over $3.5 million (he is yet another rags-to-riches Spokane statistic). It is said he would generously and innocently offer money to local women who fell into hard times and prostitution in order to help them start a new and better life for themselves.

In 1883–84, Cannon set out to build one of the city's grandest mansions ever for his family. The four-story Victorian was a jaw dropper. It was the first home in Spokane that boasted central heating and gas lighting. To accommodate the ladies, he had custom mahogany bathtubs made with tin linings and a Steinway grand piano placed in the foyer. Even the horse stables were elaborate and made from mahogany! In front of his estate, Spokane had another first—a beautiful water fountain feature.

In 1888, his lovely mansion was robbed. A year later, a fire burned down his bank. His last hope of better circumstances halted abruptly as the financial Panic of 1893 came upon Spokane. Now the hard times fell on Cannon himself. To his despair, he lost pretty much everything.

Cannon launched a newspaper called the *Spokane Chronicles*. His rival and enemy Francis Cook had a competing paper called the *Spokane Times*. The men quarreled often, and they even stooped to a fistfight that turned into a gun fight that left them both arrested on charges of attempted murder. Much to Cannon's delight, the lead juror in the case was his best friend, James Glover.

He remarried after his first wife died but tried to keep the second marriage secret. In 1894, a headline in the *Seattle Post-Intelligencer* asked, "Is Mr. Cannon Married?" This caused quite a stir, and Cannon made a public statement in December: "To the manager of the *Review*, Rumors have reached me that I have been recently married. They are absolutely false. Make a statement to that effect. A.M. Cannon."

Yet in January, a New York newspaper received a telegram with a copy of Cannon's marriage license to Eleanor Ward dated December 11, 1893. He finally fessed up. It is possible he wanted to keep the marriage a secret because he met Ward while his first wife was still alive.

Cannon unfortunately died penniless in a hotel in New York City. The "father" of Spokane's body was honorably brought back to Spokane, his beloved town, and buried in the Greenwood Cemetery.

No one really knows how many spirits haunt the Greenwood Cemetery, but it could be any number of old pioneers. Paranormal investigators claim they record the voices of many spirits and often see apparitions. The mausoleum remains vacant but is a cold and silent reminder of years gone past and all the men who helped to create Spokane.

NOTE: The haunted stairs and mausoleum are now located on private property. Please ask for permission to visit the site. The concrete stairs are in bad shape and dangerous. Security officers patrol the grounds after dusk, so do not plan to visit after hours, as you will not be allowed and asked to leave.

Browne's Addition

A Beautiful and Haunted Neighborhood

Many buildings in the area known as Browne's Addition are reported to be haunted. It is unclear why so much paranormal activity exists there. The beautiful Patsy Clark Mansion, the Campbell House and many more are inhabited by spirits. Browne's Addition is known as Spokane's oldest and most historic neighborhoo and one of the most well-loved areas in the region. It is listed in both the Spokane Historical Register as well as the National Historic Register. The 120-plus acres were platted in the 1880s by A.M. Cannon and John Browne, a well-respected lawyer from Portland, Oregon. John J. Browne was an Oregon Trail pioneer whose dealings in real estate eventually gave the neighborhood its name.

In 1870, Browne and Cannon purchased 120 acres with the dreams of developing the land, which they eventually did, creating Spokane's first truly established neighborhood. Thus the names Browne's Addition and Cannon Addition evolved. In 1888, the men developed a street-drawn horse carriage transportation business that would carry people from their neighborhood to downtown Spokane.

So why does the Browne's Addition area seem to have so much paranormal activity? The creepier side of the Browne's neighborhood history is that Browne unknowingly plowed over an old cemetery during construction of one of his projects—the rotting remains of many coffins and bones were found.

In was recently discovered that a cemetery from 1883 *did* exist at that location and that the bones were that of multiple early pioneers. Others speculate the skeletons were that of several early Native Americans from the Spokane tribe. Although most of the graves were carefully relocated, some unfortunately were left behind.

In 1910, a few more coffins were unburied and again in 1987 several more unknown skeletons were unearthed. No wonder the area is haunted. The 1987 bones were dug up at an area known as the Ridge. The Ridge once was part of the historic Cowles Mansion property, among a few others. William Hutchinson Cowles (1866–1946) moved to Spokane from Illinois and became a prominent player in the formation and success of the *Spokesman-Review* newspaper. He was also a founding member of the Spokane Chamber of Commerce and a regional director for the Boy Scouts of America. The Cowles family still runs the newspaper and has many real estate interests in Spokane.

Spokane's Shadow People

Another Spokane urban legend is that of the mysterious Shadow People that can often be seen lurking around the Browne's Addition area and parts of downtown. These mysterious creatures have much speculation about their existence. Are they just folklore? Are they part of some strange underground group of homeless people?

There *are* underground tunnels throughout Spokane that were used in the old days for steam pipes and other maintenance. But the phenomena of Shadow People are not limited to Spokane. The mysterious sightings of these dark, misty figures create quite a stir. Some believe they are nothing more than a person's overactive imagination (especially at night when alone). Others feel they are the product of astral bodies or the residue from people who are experiencing out-of-body incidents. Still others believe they are some part of the time traveler phenomena. We may never know, as they happen so quickly and without any warning whatsoever, capturing them on camera or video is next to impossible.

MINNEHAHA PARK

Ghosts of Children Still Play There

A ghost story from Cheryl of Spokane:
I was walking through the park area and just a few other people were there, and I thought I heard a child kinda cry out. I turned around thinking maybe some kid fell off a bike or whatever, but I didn't see a child anywhere. Then the sounds of muffled laughs like they were poking fun at me or something. It wasn't really scary it was more surreal. Strange.

Once the summer home of a gentleman lawyer named Edgar Jerome Webster (1847–1939), the area has been reportedly haunted for many years. Voices and laughter from children can be heard when no one is around. The sounds of children's footsteps can be heard when none are playing on the grounds. Rumors that the old stone building was once an orphanage and that the unwanted children were killed is false. Another rumor of a tragic fire that took the lives of several children is also false. So where do these paranormal sounds come from? No one knows exactly.

Webster was born in Michigan in 1847. Both he and his father served in the Fourth Michigan Volunteer Infantry. At the Battle of Cold Harbor, Edgar was tragically shot in both of his legs, leaving him partially crippled for three years. Against the odds, in 1870 he became the youngest deputy in Michigan. He later traveled through all of California, South and Central America and then Mexico. In 1882, he moved to Spokane to practice law. At that time, Spokane had a mere seven hundred residents. Soon he lost interest in his legal practices and instead concentrated on both real estate and mining adventures. This was a great move on his part. Soon he was invested in the profitable Ross Park Street Railroad Company and the Fairmont Cemetery Association. He was also president of the Gentlemen's Business Club of Spokane. Webster discovered mineral springs on his property and in the 1890s turned the property into a healing spa. As the owner and president of his thirty-acre Minnehaha Springs and Health Resort, he branched out into other business ventures that included his beneficial spring water. Webster was not a greedy man, and he felt his pure spring water should be available to the public. He sincerely felt that his Minnehaha water was the purest water available to mankind and that it could cure many ails. He even had it tested by the famous water analysis chemist Walter S. Haines from the Rush Medical College in Chicago. A promotional ad he ran in the *Spokane Daily Chronicle* in 1893 boasted that he also offered for sale his concoctions of ginger ale, champagne cider, orange soda, banana soda and chocolate soda, along with other flavors. He boasted, "I have spared no time or money in bringing these goods to a high state of perfection!"

Webster did so much to forward the city of Spokane and invested so much money in local real estate and businesses it is a shame that he is not more well known. He owned many large real estate holdings and development additions as well as five hundred acres on the riverfront and so much more. He loved Spokane and wanted to do everything in his power to make the city a success.

Later he sold his springs property to a man named John Heiber, who had the brilliant idea to use the excellent water for his brewery. In 1909, the city of Spokane purchased the thirty-nine acres in the hopes of developing a park. Until the plans for a park became reality in 1934, the land was used for the location of several movies. In 1918, the silent movie *Fool's Gold* was filmed at Minnehaha Park; then in 1923 the movie *Grub Stake* was filmed there.

Spokane is no stranger to being the location for several scenes in many movies, including:

- *Vision Quest* (1985) with Madonna
- *Benny & Joon* (1993) with Johnny Depp
- *Mozart and the Whale* (2005) with Josh Hartnett and Radha Mitchell
- *The Cutter* (2005) with Chuck Norris
- *End Game* (2006) with Burt Reynolds
- *Home of the Brave* (2006) with Jessica Biel and Christina Ricci

As interesting as the Hollywood history is, the child-like hauntings of Minnehaha Park remain a mystery. Perhaps a new movie about the ghosts of little children can be shot there, and perhaps a few real ghosts will appear in the film.

A Murdered Bodyguard at Minnehaha

One of the spirits that might be haunting Minnehaha Park is the victim of foul play in the fall of 1909. The mangled body of an Italian bodyguard named Ernest Santaro was found stabbed twenty-one times on the grounds of Minnehaha. The good-looking Italian man was hired as a bodyguard for a mobster named Frank Bruno. Bruno had a long history of marital and financial troubles, and it was reported that he at one time even hired a hit man to kill his wife. Fortunately, she was only shot in the leg and survived.

On the fateful night of Santaro's death, Bruno and Santaro were drinking at the saloon located at Front Street and Browne; then they returned to Bruno's house near Minnehaha Park around 7:30 p.m. Santaro was attacked sometime after that, after he left Bruno's home to return to his own place in the Hillyard area. Earlier that evening, a group of men were fighting in front of the saloon where the men were drinking, but if that coincidence is part of Santaro's fate, the world will never know.

Santaro was found dead with eight knife wounds in his chest, four in his neck and another nine between his shoulders. An old Italian custom is one knife wound for each husband Santaro had wronged by sleeping with their wives—more likely Santaro made someone angry, and this was just a violent payback.

Either way, Santaro's spirit could be lingering at the park still planning his revenge on his killer.

NOTE: Directions from the Washington Trails Association. From downtown Spokane, take I-90 and drive east, then take Exit 282 for Trent Avenue and Hamilton Street. Follow Hamilton Street north for .5 miles to Mission Street and take a right. Head east for less than a mile to the railroad crossing and then take a left on Upriver Drive. Follow this road for 3.3 miles along the Spokane River to a stop sign. Make a right and drive 0.1 miles to the parking area.

MONROE STREET BRIDGE

A Worker Still Cries for Help

The Monroe Street Bridge at 218 North Monroe Street was built in 1910–11 by famous architects Kirtland Cutter and Karl Malmgren. It is still classified as a beautiful city landmark. In 1911, the 281-foot-long center span concrete bridge was the largest in the United States and third longest in the world.

The project was not a simple one, and workers were held by cables over the swift, raging river, making the task even more perilous. The freezing waters below ran 140 feet deep and 1,500 wide and flowed at an incredible 40,000 cubic feet per second.

First, they had to tear down the original bridge, built in 1891, which without warning collapsed a one-hundred-foot area on the south bank. Then an extremely violent windstorm in July brought more trouble and problems. During this troublesome phase is probably when the two workers were tragically killed (George Parr and Carl Bentson or Benkson), and reportedly they still haunt the bridge.

The project exceeded the original cost and finally reached over a $500,000 reportedly half of which went toward labor (but this could be disputed). Labor rates in 1911 for the men were just $3.50 per day (later increased to $5.00 per day), with common labor being $2.75 per day increased to $3.00 per day.

One particular addition to the bridge's construction was the ornate bison skulls added to the sides of the four pavilions. Eight beautiful skulls in total adorn the bridge. The reason for adding these creative bison skulls is unclear. Original drawings submitted show American Indians with canoe designs on the pavilions and bison skulls located under the arches. Cutter and Malmgren's drawing showed the bison skulls attached where they currently

Top: The Monroe Street Bridge looking east with the churning river below where two men lost their lives and continue to haunt the water. *Washington State Archives.*

Bottom: The original Monroe Bridge, now rebuilt and haunted by two workers who died during construction. *Spokane Public Library.*

are. The symbolism of the skulls is also unclear, but Cutter remarked in 1973 that the skulls were "installed for personal reasons," possibly inspiration gathered from his visit to Montana.

The bridge was christened on November 11, 1911, and over three thousand people showed up for the event. It was listed in the National Register of Historic Places in 1976.

A Murdered Policeman

Although the legend goes that the Monroe Street Bridge is haunted by an unknown worker who died during its construction, it may actually be haunted by a murdered policeman named William Cook. Cook was a Spokane deputy who went missing for two months. Cook was last seen at the State Armory Hall at 202 West Second Street on January 21, 1909. Unfortunately, his body was found by a man named Joe Heffner floating months later in the river near the foot of Oak Street. Cook's coat and gold watch were missing, which suggested his death may have been brought on by robbery. They only found his identification and seventy-five cents on his body. Although Cook had suffered several wounds to his head, the coroner decided his death was actually due to drowning. His body was held at Gilman Undertaking until his funeral, and the killer was never found.

Perhaps Deputy Cook's killer was one of the men who, at the Cooks' home earlier that year, proceeded to fight with Mr. and Mrs. Cook under the influence of alcohol. It was reported in the *Spokane Press* that Jacob Hargert proceeded to brawl with Cook and then gave the man several blows to his head with a hammer. The other man, Conrad Lind, tried to assault Mrs. Cook. The two men were charged with the assaults, but maybe they took out their revenge on Cook for pressing charges and killed him? Some dead bodies never tell their secrets.

NOTE: Another local legend is that a depressed priest hanged himself from the Monroe Bridge and his spirit haunts the area, but no evidence has been found about this suicide.

THE HAUNTED INTERSECTION

The Corner of Death Is Still Feared

An odd paranormal location is an intersection at Division and Sprague that has earned the nickname "Death Corner." It is where a group of Spokane streets are divided all four ways—north, south, east and west—and an unlucky area to be avoided at all costs.

The gruesome story behind the hauntings begins on September 6, 1890, when two hundred pounds of dynamite exploded during a Northern Pacific

Railroad freight yard project. The job included the dangerous duty of removing a twenty-foot-high rock cliff and ledge—and thirty unlucky men were working directly underneath it when the terrible explosion occurred. Considered one of Spokane's deadliest tragedies, these thirty men lost their lives in a single instant, along with dozens of horses that were being worked to pull out the debris. Due to the extreme damage caused by over twenty-five thousand cubic feet of falling rocks crashing down in a flash, only fifteen of the thirty bodies could actually be recovered. The weight of the falling rocks made some of the bodies and a few horses nothing more than a memory.

Countless other workers were badly injured. Sadly, the actual names of many men were never revealed, as many immigrant men were "nameless"; they were often identified by only a number on a metal tag while on the job. During these times, men could drift and find odd jobs signing in and out with an X or an assigned number. Some could not speak English or were evading the police but were willing to put in hard labor, so they were hired.

On this particular horrific and tragic evening, the dynamite was routinely placed and scheduled to detonate at exactly 6:00 p.m., after most of the crew would have left for the day. But when the dynamite accidentally discharged twenty minutes early, the earth-shattering explosion caught all of the men off guard. Instead of heading home for the evening to spend time with their loved ones, they would never see their families again.

Foreman James McPherson and powder man Joseph Rhea were tamping the dynamite when it went off unexpectedly, killing both men instantly. During the long and careful three hours of the laborious and sickening rescue efforts by brave men, nerves were rattling as other charges were still in place and could go off at any minute, killing more men.

Many of the men who died were hardworking, poor immigrants from all over the world. They were housed in a lower end section of Spokane termed "Shantytown." Not all of the workers were known by their real names, and many were identified by a number on a brass tag.

Their bodies were buried in a mass grave plot at Greenwood Memorial Terrace. In honor of the men who lost their lives, a monument was placed near the graves by the Fairmount Memorial Association in 1996. In honor of the men who were killed, a list of twenty-four known names has been compiled here: Henry Aptill, Louis Arlett, James Ballane, Henry Cobini, John Courtland, Nicola Dimottes, R. Erickson, August Fluron, Hugh Hayes, Jacob Hemine, F.A. Holm, Isaac Johnson, Gust Julien, Thomas Maher,

William Maunsel, James McPherson, Home Oleson, Ray Pinkney, Andrew Puelonelio, Peter Raffalle, Joseph Rhea, James Tablo, Raffel Vetter and August Warm. The name John Castner also comes up as one of the victims.

May all of the brave men and horses who died so tragically on that day rest in peace.

HELEN APARTMENTS

A Serial Killer Gets Caught

Perhaps one of the most gruesome haunts in Spokane is the site where forty-six-year-old convicted killer Stanley Pietrzak murdered a young woman and possibly killed others. Paranormal activity consists of rumors of phantom screams coming from the basement in this building, the smell of a burning fire when there is no fire and undeniable cold spots. Luckily, concerned citizens and other tenants were able to bring justice for his victim and possibly saved other people from the same terrible fate by going to the police.

Working as the manager of the apartments on the northeast corner of Adams and Second Avenue from 1997 to 1998, Pietrzak lured victim Kelly Conway into his apartment. Conway was partially disabled and lived in the apartment building. A small group would occasionally get together and drink and watch TV. The night of her death, it was documented that she was complaining of a backache. Pietrzak offered her some pills to relieve her pain. The others finally went back to their own apartments, leaving Conway to her untimely and unfortunate demise.

Conway was last seen alive that November night in 1998.

In the spring of 1999, police got a tip to search the basement for Conway's remains. Apparently, Pietrzak had been bragging about killing her and even went so far as professing cannibalism. He told people that she was "better off dead." This too got back to the police. The police quickly arrested Pietrzak.

After he was convicted of first-degree murder, Pietrzak testified that he did *not* kill her but simply "woke up and found her dead in his bed." He panicked and after a few days reportedly dismembered her body and burned her in the basement furnace. But the evidence found in the basement told another story—one so horrible it is hard to comprehend.

After the autopsy, forensic pathologist Dr. George Lindholm ruled Conway's death an absolute homicide. Pietrzak was sentenced to a mere forty years, and the system suffered his many appeals.

It is interesting that Karen Pietrzak, his former wife, died in a suspiciously similar manner in Pietrzak's bed in 1976. Another woman, Allison Weaver, was found dead in his bed in 1998. Coincidence? Not likely.

The building is now renovated, but mysterious sounds can still be heard coming from inside. It is a relief to know Pietrzak is locked up and cannot hurt any more innocent women even if his victims' souls are still angry from beyond the grave.

FORT GEORGE WRIGHT

The Spot of Many Murders and Wounded Soldiers

The new Fort Wright was built in 1898 in order to replace three older forts in the area: Spokane, Walla Walla and Sherman. Even though it could hold only twenty-four prisoners, many murders occurred there.

It housed thousands of soldiers over the years, including the famous Buffalo Soldiers. Men from the Spanish-American War, both World Wars I and II and the Korean War were stationed at Fort Wright. In 1941, it officially became a U.S. Air Force base, and then three years later it became a convalescent hospital for wounded soldiers. During this time, the fort/hospital developed an incredible program for healing that included music (performed by the 707th Army Air Force band), many art programs and working with the livestock on the land. In 1949, it changed again and became the Fort George Wright Air Force Base but closed its doors in 1957. In 1960, the building went under the control of the Sisters of the Holy Name Convent and was turned into a college. After some financial troubles, the building was purchased in 1990 and used as a Japanese girls' college.

Later it was used for student housing, and rumors persisted that the souls of war victims could be seen roaming the grounds and their screaming voices could be heard late at night. Is it possible the hauntings are caused by wounded soldiers? Or maybe the hauntings are from the 1916 murder of a thirty-five-year-old Indian woman named Alice Vivian. A man named Edward Mayberry confronted Alice and demanded she go with him somewhere. She refused. In a fit of rage, he killed her on the Colville Indian Reservation. He fled the crime scene but was soon captured by two local farmers, Thomas Dennen and Barney Dickson. Mayberry was put in jail with a $5,000 bail over his head.

Aerial shot of Fort George Wright, haunted by several interesting entities. *Washington State Archives.*

Mayberry was found guilty and sentenced to death and scheduled to be hanged in April 1917. Mayberry would be the only Washington resident to be hanged during the years 1913 to 1919. Does his trapped soul haunt the fort to this day? Or is it haunted by some of the soldiers or prisoners?

Three Bullets to the Head

Another possibility is the grounds of Fort Wright are haunted by a man murdered by someone he thought was his friend in 1909.

The unfortunate victim, a Polish cabinetmaker named Paul Lewandowski (also spelled Saudawaski and Kravsanowski and first name also Jan or John), was murdered by another Polish immigrant in Spokane named Paul Clein (who also went by the alias H.W. Wilson and was a former officer in a European army) sometime during the early part of May. His body wasn't found until several weeks later.

Sergeant Lathoff of Fort Wright stumbled upon the victim lying in some brush in a nearby field. He had three bullet wounds to his head. It appeared the perpetrator had tried to burn his victim's body and thus the evidence. The murderer was found out; he carelessly kept thirty dollars and a coat that were stolen from Lewandowski. Of course, Clein claimed he was innocent.

The trial became a Spokane sensation and garnered much publicity. Lies, ongoing witnesses, false alibis, bribery as well as a fiancée and girlfriend all got involved. But the evidence stacked up against Clein.

A young livery boy named Glen Smith who worked at the O.K. Stables testified that Clein had rented a black horse and yellow-trimmed buggy at 9:30 p.m. the night in question and borrowed the horse for several hours. Several witnesses claimed to have seen Clein driving this buggy through Coopertown and into the area where the body was found.

A sixty-two-year-old woman named Ella Newkirk heard gunshots coming from the direction of the reservation late on the evening of March 1. She testified, "The shots were followed by two awful screams that made a chill come over me."

George Croling saw Clein driving the same buggy the early morning of the second going through Coopertown. He insisted that Clein was the driver. He later saw the same horse and buggy stopped in the area where the body was found.

But the game was up when Sergeant Lathoff, in full uniform, recalled he had also seen Clein and the buggy on the grounds where the body was found. Clein was arrested at the Lynne Hotel.

Paul Lewandowski, angry by the betrayal of his friend who took his life for a mere thirty dollars, could definitely by the spirit who haunts the Fort George Wright location.

NOTE: At the nearby Fort George Wright Cemetery overlooking the Spokane River, many of the trees planted there are labeled Gettysburg Address Sycamores. These trees are grown from the actual sycamore trees that grow at the original site of the Gettysburg battlefield. History lives on.

HORSE SLAUGHTER CAMP

Phantom Cries from Horses and Indians

Colonel George Wright (1803–1865) was a ruthless commander and has gone down in Spokane's history for more than just fighting wars. He brought such devastation to an area on the east side of the Spokane River that it is said to be haunted to this day—by both Indians and almost one thousand slaughtered horses. The cries of mares losing their foals and of Indians losing their herd still ring in the air.

Left: A rare photograph of Colonel George Wright, 1855. *Washington State Archives.*

Below: Unidentified men and Indians on their horses in the Spokane Valley in 1868. Some believe the valley is haunted by the many Indians and eight-hundred-plus horses that lost their lives during the war period. *Library of Congress.*

Wright originally joined the army in 1882 and fought the Battle of Veracruz and Molino del Rey during the Mexican-American War in 1858. The horrific saga of Horse Slaughter Camp began when the local Indians killed two prospectors who were on their land. Lieutenant Colonel Edward Steptoe (1816–1865) was sent to investigate this matter, which quickly turned into a ten-hour battle. On the eleventh hour, Steptoe retreated.

Wright decided that he would punish the Indians and make them starve. So in retaliation against the tribes, Wright demanded that his soldiers

The land by Colonel Wright's horse slaughter camp on the Spokane River in 1858; around nine hundred Indian horses were killed over a three-day period. *Spokane Public Library, photographer Frank Palmer.*

capture and kill the Indian horses that were peacefully grazing along the river. It took his men two days to kill the innocent animals. Wright believed the best way to cripple the Palouse and Nez Perce tribes was to take away their herd of horses. If that was not bad enough, Wright also ordered the hanging of sixteen Indian warriors (who had already surrendered) at what was later to be termed Hangman's Creek. It is recorded that Wright did not actually even have the authority to make the decision to carry through with the hangings.

Wright wrote in a journal: "I deeply regretted killing these poor creatures, but a dire necessity drove me to it." He also wrote: "The chastisement which these Indians have received has been severe but well merited and absolutely necessary to impress them with our power. A blow has been struck which they will never forget."

The Indians watched with sheer horror and disbelief at what was happening to their horses from a nearby hill. The killing of the horses was to prevent further warfare by the Indians, but it was senseless due to the fact that the war was basically already over anyway. The bones lay by the river for many years to come, a silent and gruesome reminder of the horrible battle that took place so long ago.

If anything is haunting the field, later known as Old Murphy's Farm, it would be the spirits of the poor horses and the betrayed local Indians. In honor of these fallen horses, a stone monument was erected in 1946 to mark the site.

NOTE: The eight-foot-tall granite monument is found at approximately mile marker no. 2 on the Centennial Trail near the Washington/Idaho border, just one mile west of the Gateway Park Visitor Center off I-90 at exit 299.

In Conclusion

The dead are watching, whether or not we choose to listen to their stories.
—*Colin Dickey,* Ghostland: An American History in Haunted Places

Stories of ghosts, hauntings and restless spirits have been around for centuries, and they will continue until the end of time. Perhaps people are fascinated by spirits because they want some sort of proof that there is life after death; they desire to know their loved ones are not suffering, or they simply think the paranormal is interesting.

As technology advances, the desire to capture proof of the existence of the afterlife has increased dramatically and is no longer limited to Ouija boards, crystal balls, tea leaves, psychics and slate writers. People no longer frown on those who choose to believe in ghosts and the spirit world; in the past, most thought it was all hoaxes and make-believe. It is now common to hear conversations about ghosts and spirits almost everywhere you go. Hundreds of paranormal groups are popping up all over the place, their members eager to prove the existence of ghosts and visit haunted places.

I am hoping the mixture of local history and hauntings in my books continue to enrich readers' lives and encourage others to explore the various places revealed herein.

I am glad to have many teachers and parents thank me for my books and tell me that they cannot get their children to take the time to read or even have the slightest interested in learning about history but that my books have opened the door for both of these things. I was once told that there was a

The serene Spokane Falls area in 1880 with Falls View Hotel visible through trees on right. To the left is Captain Jenkins's white house. *Spokane Public Library, photographer W.E. Wing.*

wait list of over seventy-six students for my book at the local library—for that, I am proud and happy. (Of course, I immediately donated a dozen more books to shorten their wait.)

And as locals and tourists roam in and out of Spokane stores and structures or enjoy a libation in an old hotel or bar, I hope that they find these tales from the past fascinating, frightening and intriguing. I also hope this book makes them stop in the entryways of the historic Davenport Hotel or the Patsy Clark mansion as they walk through old buildings and cemeteries and ponder the past. Maybe they will pause for just a second or two to remember those early Spokane pioneers who worked so hard to create the wonderful town that everyone loves today.

And who knows, maybe they will even spot a dark apparition lurking in a corner somewhere or hear the faint whispers of a restless ghost asking for help. Better yet, they will feel the lightest touch of a cold hand as a ghost tries to caress the side of their face as they slowly turn to walk away.

Happy hauntings!

SOURCES

Ancestry.com.

Arksey, Laura. "Great Spokane Fire Destroys Downtown Spokane Falls on August 4, 1889." History Link. https://www.historylink.org/File/7696.

Bamonte, Suzanne, Tony Bamonte and the Spokane Police Department. Life Behind the Badge. Spokane, WA: Tornado Creek Publications, 2008.

Downtown Spokane Heritage Walk. http://www.historicspokane.org/HeritageTours/downtown.

The Famous People. "Bing Crosby Biography." https://www.thefamouspeople.com/profiles/bing-crosby-3328.php.

Find a Grave. "Edgar Jerome Webster." https://www.findagrave.com/memorial/104235218/edgar-jerome-webster.

Historical Reflections of the Davenport Hotel. https://davenportreflections.wordpress.com/tag.

Influenza Encyclopedia. www.influenzaarchive.org.

Lynden Tribune. "Ridpath Arrested." January 9, 1913.

McClary, Daryl C. "George Webster Is Hanged for First-Degree Murder at Spokane County Courthouse on March 30, 1900." History Link. https://www.historylink.org/File/10258.

Newport Miner. "William Ridpath for Congress." August 29, 1912.

Nillson, Lee. "Frontier Justice at Fort George Wright." Spokane Historical Society. https://spokanehistorical.org/items/show/175.

———. "Welcome to Historic Fort George Wright." Spokane Historical Society. https://spokanehistorical.org/items/show/173.

Richards, John H. *The Life and Times of Patsy Clark: Mining Pioneer*. Spokane, WA: Gray Dog Press, 2018.

Russell, Julie Y. "A History of Greenwood Cemetery," Spokane Historical. https://spokanehistorical.org/items/show/125.

Seattle Post Intelligencer. "Happy on the Gibbet." September 7, 1892.

Seattle Times. "Apartment Manager Found Guilty of Murder." August 23, 2000.

Spokane City | County Historic Preservation Office. Historic Properties of Spokane nomination applications for the National Historic Register. https://properties.historicspokane.org.

Spokane Press. "Indian Scared Sheep; Was Killed in Caliboose." March 13, 1910.

———. "She Heard Shots." May 28, 1909.

Spokesman (Spokane, WA). "Many Are Dead." September 7, 1890.

Tacoma Times. "Murder Mystery." March 27, 1909.

Visit Spokane. visitspokane.com.

Wikipedia. "John R. Monaghan." https://en.wikipedia.org/w/index.php?title=John_R._Monaghan&oldid=875402668.

About the Author

Originally from Ithaca in upstate New York, Deborah Cuyle loves everything about small towns. She has also written *Kidding Around Portland* (OR), Images of America: *Cannon Beach* (OR), *Haunted Snohomish* (WA), *Ghosts of Leavenworth and the Cascade Foothills* (WA), *Haunted Everett* (WA), *Ghosts of Coeur d'Alene and the Silver Valley* (ID) and *The 1910 Wellington Disaster* (WA). Coming soon: *Ghosts and Legends of Spokane* (WA), *Murder and Mayhem in Spokane* (WA), *Wicked Coeur d'Alene* (ID), *Ghostly Tales of Snohomish* (WA) and *Murder and Mayhem in Coeur d'Alene* (ID). Her passions include local history, animals, museums, hiking and horseback riding. Deborah enjoys thinking about the possibility of an afterlife and especially loves telling a chilling ghost story while nestled beside a bonfire with her best friends and family. She and her husband are currently remodeling a haunted house in Wallace, Idaho, and a former funeral home built in 1881 in South Dakota.

Visit us at
www.historypress.com